Holidays In Cross-Stitch

1995

Oxmoor House.

©1994 by Oxmoor House, Inc.
Book Division of Southern Progress Corporation
P.O. Box 2463, Birmingham, AL 35201

Library of Congress Catalog Card Number: 86-62285
Hardcover ISBN: 0-8487-1407-5
Softcover ISBN: 0-8487-1406-7
ISSN: 0890-8230
Manufactured in the United States of America
First Printing 1994

Editor-in-Chief: Nancy J. Fitzpatrick
Senior Homes Editor: Mary Kay Culpepper
Senior Editor, Editorial Services: Olivia Kindig Wells
Art Director: James Boone

Holidays In Cross-Stitch 1995

Editor: Lelia Gray Neil
Editorial Assistant: Janica Lynn York
Copy Editor: L. Amanda Owens
Copy Assistant: Jennifer K. Mathews
Assistant Art Director: Cynthia R. Cooper
Designers: Diana Smith Morrison, Eleanor Cameron
Illustrator: Kelly Davis
Production and Distribution Director: Phillip Lee
Production Manager: Gail H. Morris
Associate Production Manager: Theresa L. Beste
Production Assistant: Marianne Jordan
Publishing Systems Administrator: Rick Tucker
Photographer: John O'Hagan

The photographs in this book were taken at
Trends and Traditions in
Ogden, Utah, and at the
home of Jo Packham.

The Vanessa-Ann Collection Staff

Jo Packham, *Owner*
Trice Boerens
Cherie Hanson
Susan Jorgensen
Leslie Ridenour
Nancy Whitley
Lorrie Young

Designers
Terrece Beesley
Trice Boerens
Polly Carbonari

Photographer
Ryne Hazen

Holidays In Cross-Stitch

1995

A Calendar of Contents

page 16

page 40

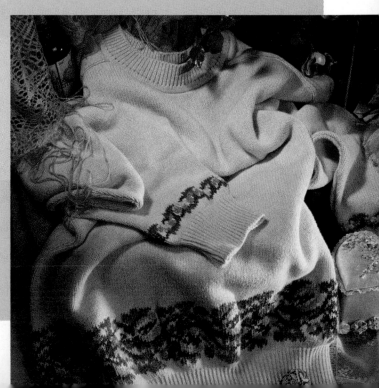

page 60

page 80

page 98

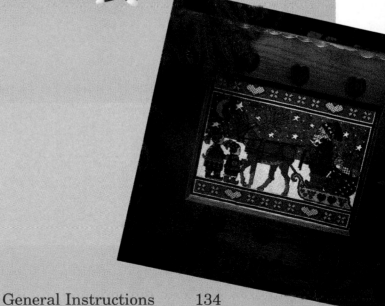

page 130

Holiday Greetings

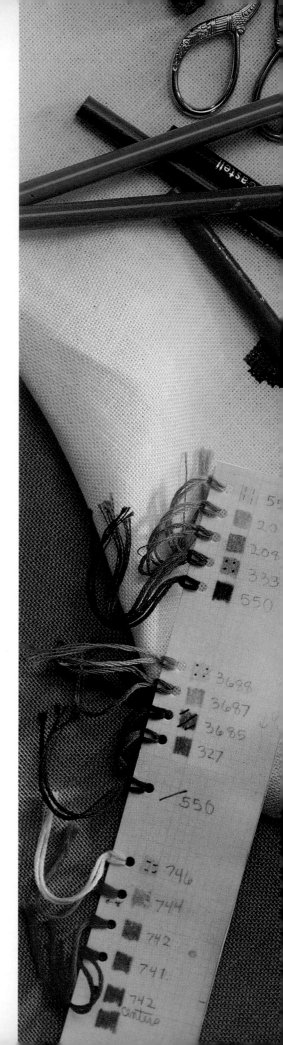

The Vanessa-Ann Collection is made up of creative people just like you. That's why we'd like to give you a glimpse into how we produce our beautiful designs.

The inspiration for our designs comes from everywhere— art books, galleries, flowers in our gardens, as well as our children. Jo Packham communicates an idea to a

Nancy Whitley and Trice Boerens

designer such as Trice Boerens. Trice draws the design on graph paper; then she and Nancy Whitley select the fabric and flosses that will best translate the work.

Jo Packham and Ryne Hazen

Once the design is stitched and finished, Jo and Ryne Hazen work their magic with the styling and photography of the project.

We hope you are as delighted with the projects in this edition of *Holidays In Cross-Stitch* as we are. From all of us at Vanessa-Ann, the best to you in the coming year.

New Year's Day

This year, turn over a new leaf with an embellished journal. Stitch one of these handsome medallions and glue it to the cover of a blank book. Then accent the stitching with a decorative gold-leaf border.

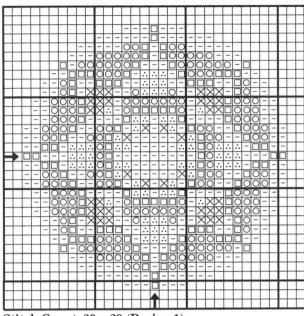

Stitch Count: 29 x 29 (Design 1)

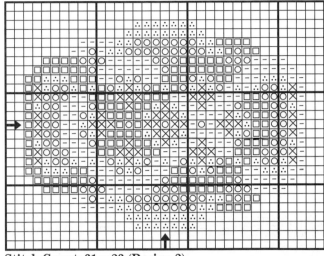

Stitch Count: 31 x 23 (Design 2)

Journal Medallions

SAMPLE for Design 1
Stitched on brown 14-count Perforated Paper, the finished design size is 2⅛" x 2⅛". The paper was cut 6" x 6". See page 135 for working with perforated paper.

FABRICS	DESIGN SIZES
11-count	2⅝" x 2⅝"
14-count	2⅛" x 2⅛"
18-count	1⅝" x 1⅝"
22-count	1⅜" x 1⅜"

SAMPLE for Design 2
Stitched on brown 14-count Perforated Paper, the finished design size is 2¼" x 1⅝". The paper was cut 6" x 6".

FABRICS	DESIGN SIZES
11-count	2⅞" x 2⅛"
14-count	2¼" x 1⅝"
18-count	1¾" x 1¼"
22-count	1⅜" x 1"

MATERIALS (for 1 journal)
Completed cross-stitch on brown 14-count Perforated Paper
Spray adhesive
Purchased journal
Gold-leaf kit (See Suppliers, page 144.)

DIRECTIONS
1. Cut out design to within ¼" of stitched area. Coat wrong side of design piece with spray adhesive. Press design piece to journal cover in desired position. Let dry.
2. Following manufacturer's instructions, use gold-leaf kit to apply sizing to outer edge of design piece, overlapping slightly onto journal cover. Sizing should cover edge of paper to within ⅛" of stitching. Press gold leaf to sizing. Let dry.

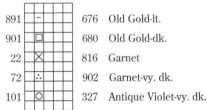

Anchor   DMC (used for sample)

Step 1: Cross-stitch (2 strands)

Anchor		DMC	
891	–	676	Old Gold-lt.
901	□	680	Old Gold-dk.
22	✕	816	Garnet
72	∴	902	Garnet-vy. dk.
101	○	327	Antique Violet-vy. dk.

BONUS STITCHES

Make a stunning pin from these old-world designs: Work a motif on 14-count Perforated Paper. Using spray adhesive, mount the finished design on mat board trimmed slightly smaller than the design piece. Glue a pin back to the mat board.

100th Anniversary of Swan Lake

On this day in 1895, Tchaikovsky's *Swan Lake* debuted in Saint Petersburg, Russia. It has since become one of the world's most beloved ballets. Your prima ballerina will adore this commemorative tote bag—it's just the thing for carrying her leotard and shoes to ballet class.

Ballet Tote Bag

SAMPLE
Stitched on white 30-count Murano over 2 threads, the finished design size is 5⅜" x 7¾". The fabric was cut 18" x 32". With design centered horizontally, begin stitching top edge of design 6" below 1 short edge of fabric. See Suppliers, page 144, for silk ribbon.

FABRICS	DESIGN SIZES
11-count	7¼" x 10½"
14-count	5¾" x 8¼"
18-count	4½" x 6½"
22-count	3⅝" x 5¼"

MATERIALS
Completed cross-stitch on white 30-count Murano; matching thread
⅛ yard unstitched white 30-count Murano
2⅓ yards 1"-wide seafoam green grosgrain ribbon; matching thread
½ yard 4-mm lilac silk ribbon
Embroidery needle

DIRECTIONS
Finished tote bag is 15" x 14¾". All seam allowances are ¼".

1. With design centered horizontally, trim design piece to

BONUS STITCHES
If you're pressed for time, stitch the design on a purchased muslin tote bag using 14-count Waste Canvas. Or appliqué the finished design piece to a heavy canvas tote. See Suppliers on page 144 for a bag.

15½" x 32". Zigzag-stitch along raw edges. With right sides facing and raw edges aligned, fold design piece in half with short ends together. Stitch side edges. Turn top edge of tote bag under ¼" and press. Then turn edge under 1" and pin.

2. Stitch diagonally across each bottom corner 1" from corner (see Diagram 1). Do not turn.

3. To make handles, cut 2 (3" x 18") strips from unstitched Murano. With right sides facing and raw edges aligned, stitch long edges of 1 strip together. Turn. Center seam and press. Repeat for other handle.

4. Referring to Diagram 2, pin 1 handle to top edge of bag, with design centered between ends of handle. Fold ends of handle ¼" under folded edge of bag. Pin remaining handle to opposite side of bag. Stitch along hem, catching ends of handles in stitching. Reinforce stitching across handles. Turn bag right side out.

5. Referring to photo and Diagram 3, attach green ribbon to bag and handles, stitching along both edges of ribbon: Beginning at bottom of bag, stitch ribbon to 1 side of bag and 1 handle. Continue around bottom of bag to attach ribbon to other side and handle. Finish at starting point, turning raw end of ribbon under.

6. Referring to photo, cut lilac ribbon in half. Using embroidery needle, stitch 1 length from heel of each shoe to palm of dancer's hand. Handling ribbons as 1, tie into bow. Trim ends if necessary.

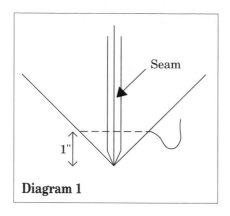
Diagram 1
Seam
1"

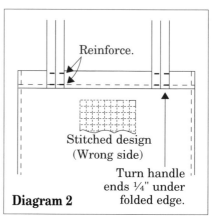
Reinforce.
Stitched design (Wrong side)
Turn handle ends ¼" under folded edge.
Diagram 2

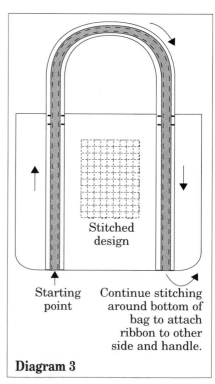
Stitched design
Starting point
Continue stitching around bottom of bag to attach ribbon to other side and handle.
Diagram 3

12

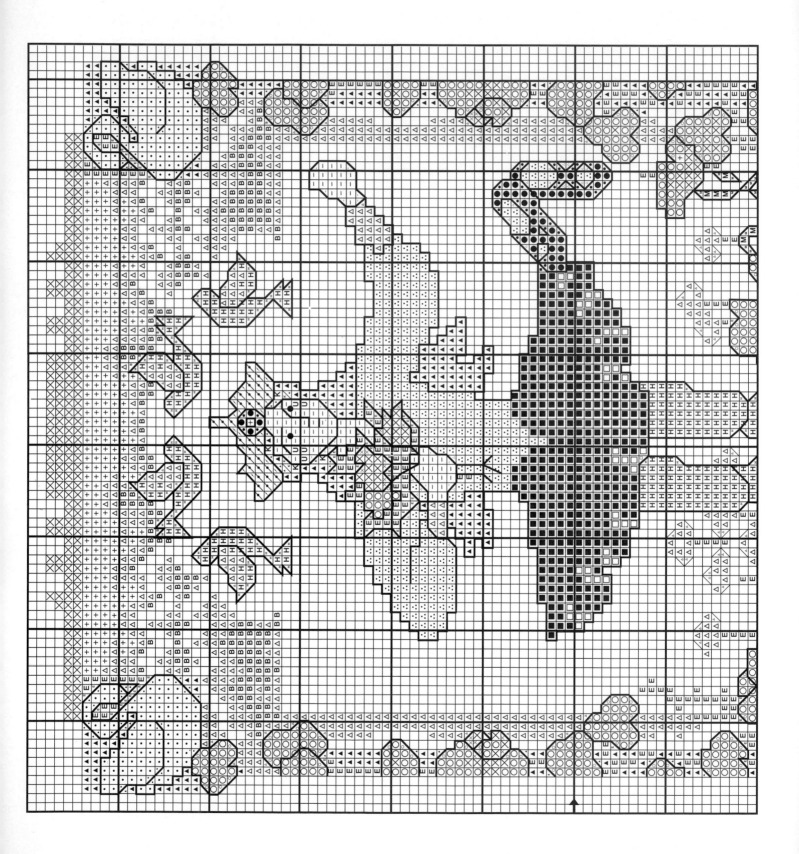

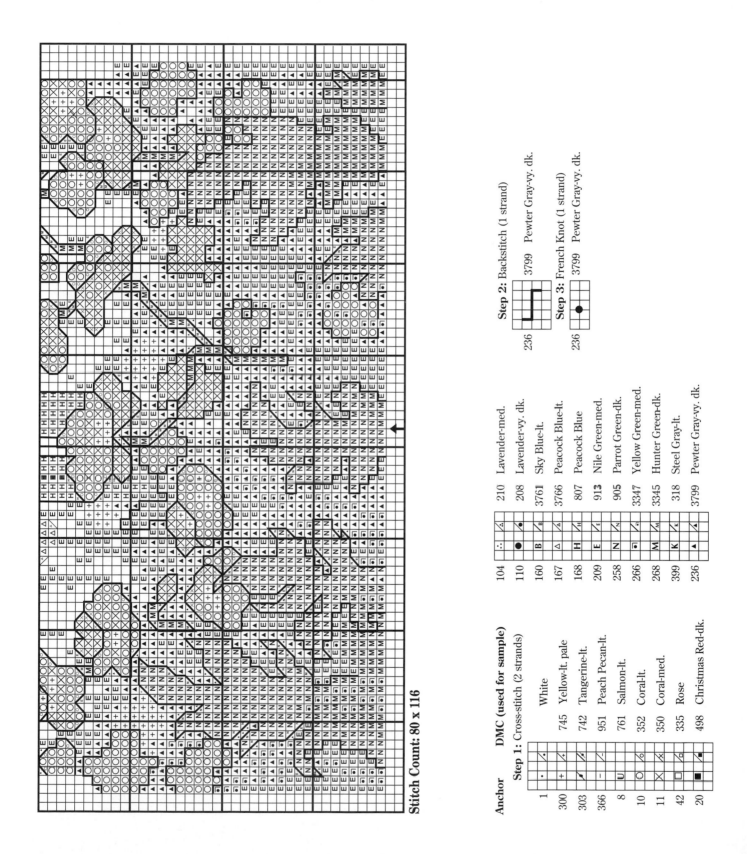

Stitch Count: 80 x 116

Anchor	DMC (used for sample)		
	Step 1: Cross-stitch (2 strands)		
1	·	∴	White
300	+	∠	745 Yellow-lt. pale
303	◢	∠	742 Tangerine-lt.
366	−	∠	951 Peach Pecan-lt.
8	U		761 Salmon-lt.
10	⌀	⌀	352 Coral-lt.
11	X	⟋	350 Coral-med.
42	▢	▫	335 Rose
20	■	◪	498 Christmas Red-dk.
104	∴	∴	210 Lavender-med.
110	●	●	208 Lavender-vy. dk.
160	B	◿	3761 Sky Blue-lt.
167	△	◹	3766 Peacock Blue-lt.
168	H	◹	807 Peacock Blue
209	E	◸	913 Nile Green-med.
258	N	◩	905 Parrot Green-dk.
266	⊡	◿	3347 Yellow Green-med.
268	M	◺	3345 Hunter Green-dk.
399	K	◹	318 Steel Gray-lt.
236	◀		3799 Pewter Gray-vy. dk.

Step 2: Backstitch (1 strand)

236		3799 Pewter Gray-vy. dk.

Step 3: French Knot (1 strand)

236	●	3799 Pewter Gray-vy. dk.

National Pie Day

On a cold winter day, nothing brightens the spirit more quickly than a piece of pie, hot from the oven. This colorfully stitched angel will enliven your breakfast room as she delivers her freshest confection.

Pie in the Sky

SAMPLE

Stitched on ash rose 30-count Murano over 2 threads, the finished design size is 4⅜" x 8⅜". The fabric was cut 11" x 15". See Framing Ideas, page 140.

FABRICS	DESIGN SIZES
11-count	5⅞" x 11⅜"
14-count	4⅝" x 8⅞"
18-count	3⅝" x 7"
22-count	3" x 5⅝"

Anchor			DMC	(used for sample)

Step 1: Cross-stitch (2 strands)

1	–	∕		White
891	N	N	676	Old Gold-lt.
901	▲	▲	680	Old Gold-dk.
297	∴	∴	743	Yellow-med.
4146	U	U	754	Peach-lt.
9	✕	✕	760	Salmon
75	□	◪	3733	Dusty Rose-lt.
20	●	●	498	Christmas Red-dk.
118	·	·	340	Blue Violet-med.
168	○	◓	807	Peacock Blue
169	W	W	806	Peacock Blue-dk.
205		◣	911	Emerald Green-med.
362	H	H	437	Tan-lt.
349	+	∕	301	Mahogany-med.
236	∕	∕	3799	Pewter Gray-vy. dk.

Step 2: Backstitch (1 strand)

236	└┐	3799	Pewter Gray-vy. dk.

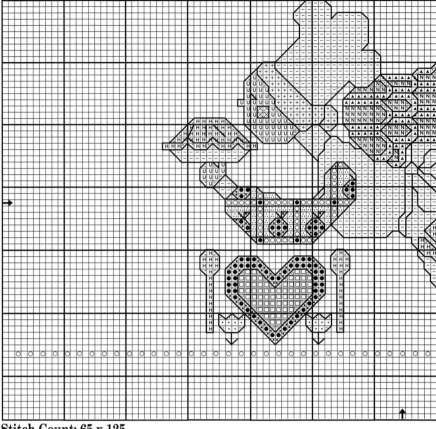

Stitch Count: 65 x 125

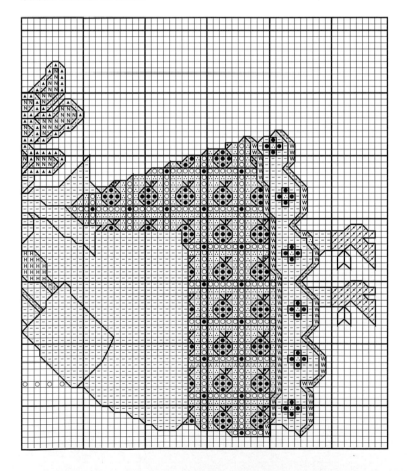

International Friendship Month

What better place to meet a good friend than over a cup of tea? Talk away—our welcoming tea cozy will keep the pot warm through a long chat.

A Warm Welcome

SAMPLE
Stitched on antique blue 28-count Linen over 2 threads, the finished design size is 12⅝" x 7¼". The fabric was cut 15" x 10".

FABRICS	DESIGN SIZES
11-count	16⅛" x 9¼"
14-count	12⅝" x 7¼"
18-count	9⅞" x 5⅝"
22-count	8" x 4⅝"

MATERIALS
Completed cross-stitch on antique blue 28-count Linen; matching thread
1 (10" x 15") piece unstitched antique blue 28-count Linen
½ yard floral print fabric; matching thread
½ yard fleece
⅞ yard ¼" cording
1 yard 1½"-wide light blue wire-edged ribbon
⅓ yard 1½-wide dark blue wire-edged ribbon
Tracing paper

DIRECTIONS
All seam allowances are ¼".
1. Transfer cozy pattern to tracing paper and cut out.

With design centered horizontally and bottom of design 1¼" above long straight edge of pattern, cut out design piece. Cut 1 cozy piece from unstitched antique blue Linen for back, 2 from print fabric for lining, and 2 from fleece.

2. From remaining print fabric, cut 1¼"-wide bias strips, piecing as needed to equal 29". Using pieced bias strip and cording, make 29" of corded piping (see page 136).

3. Baste 1 fleece piece each to wrong side of design piece and back. With raw edges aligned, stitch corded piping to right side of design piece along curved edge. With right sides facing, raw edges aligned, and piping toward center, stitch front and back together along stitching line of piping, leaving straight edge open. Trim fleece from seam allowance. Clip curves; turn.

4. To make lining, with right sides facing and raw edges aligned, stitch print fabric pieces together, leaving straight edge open and an opening on curved edge for turning. Clip curves but do not turn. With right sides facing, slide lining over cozy, matching seams. Stitch around bottom straight edge of cozy. Turn through opening in lining. Slipstitch opening closed. Tuck lining inside cozy.

5. To make ribbon rosette, run gathering thread along 1 long edge of light blue ribbon; pull to gather tightly. Roll ribbon into rosette, tacking to secure. To •make leaves, cut dark blue ribbon into 3 (4") lengths. Fold each length in half widthwise; run gathering thread across cut ends to secure. Pull each to gather; shape into leaves. Referring to photo, tack leaves and flower to center top of cozy.

BONUS STITCHES

Frame this design for a charming piece of artwork in your kitchen or breakfast nook. Or if you're in need of a hostess gift, use waste canvas to work a row of teapots across the border of a damask tea towel.

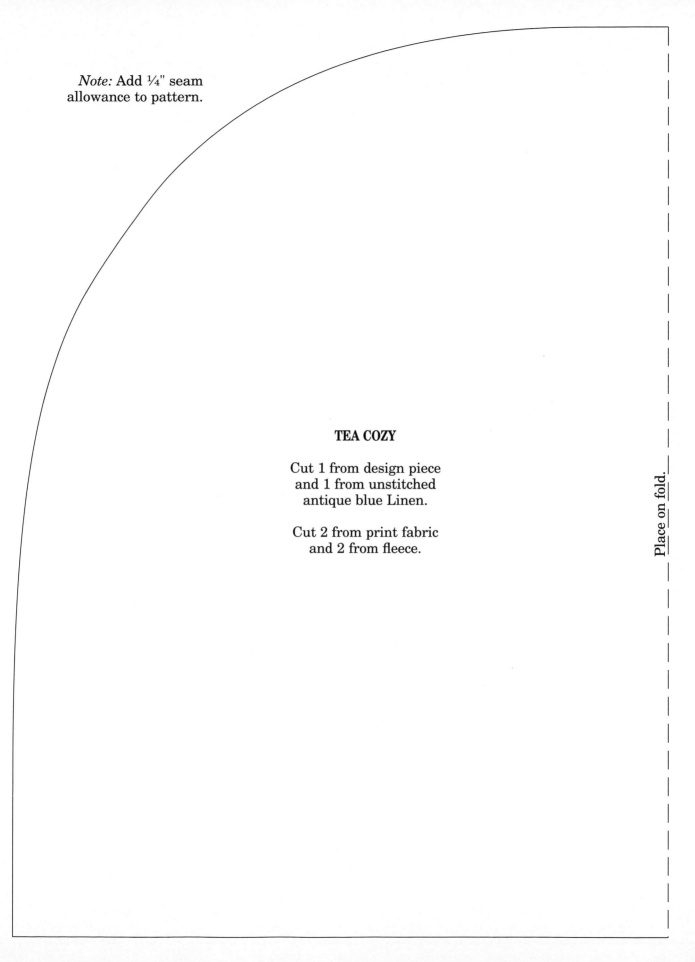

Note: Add ¼" seam allowance to pattern.

TEA COZY

Cut 1 from design piece and 1 from unstitched antique blue Linen.

Cut 2 from print fabric and 2 from fleece.

Place on fold.

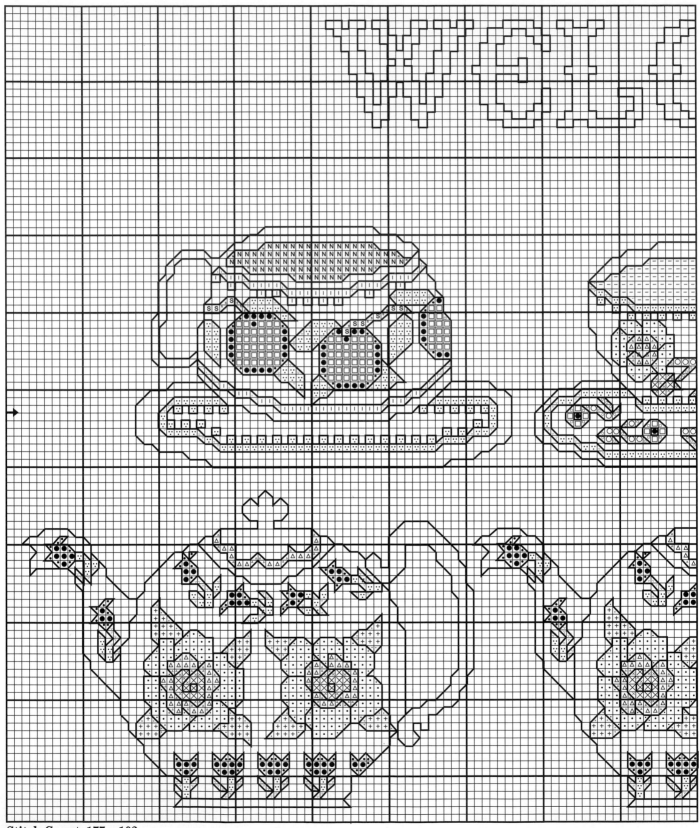

Stitch Count: 177 x 102

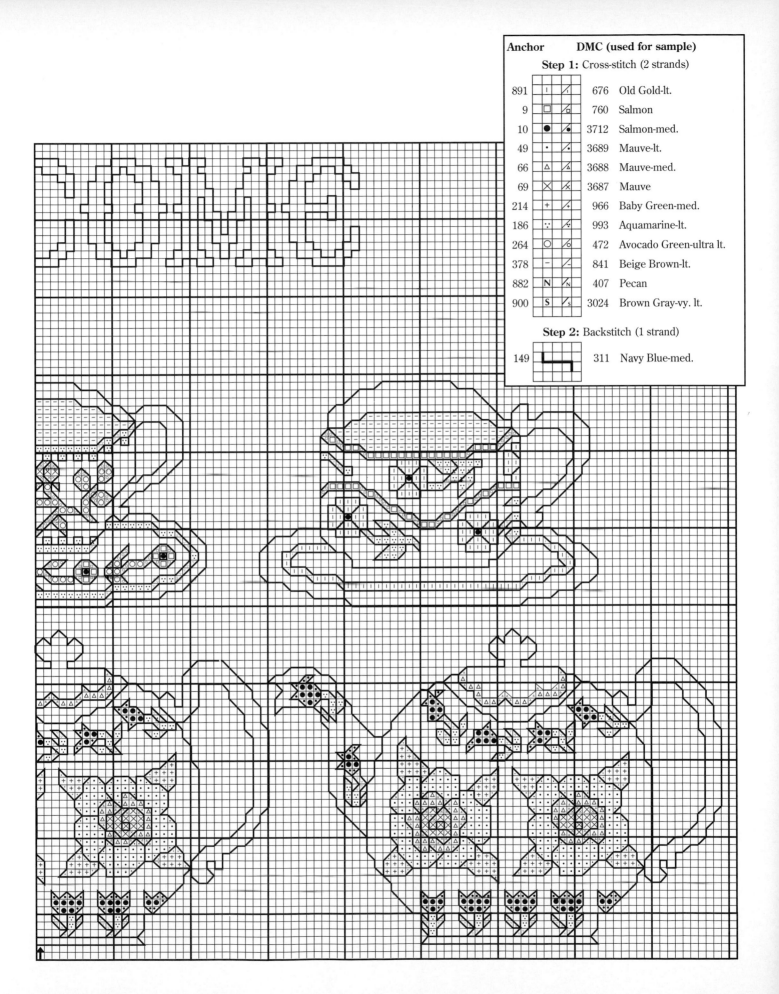

National Cherry Month

No wonder they say that "life is just a bowl of cherries," for life is

vivid and sweet, just like this cross-stitched sweatshirt.

Stitch Count: 79 x 79

Cherry Sweatshirt

SAMPLE
Stitched with 10-count Waste Canvas on a purchased sweatshirt, the finished design size is 7⅞" x 7⅞". The canvas was cut 9" x 9". See page 135 for working with waste canvas.

FABRICS	DESIGN SIZES
11-count	7⅛" x 7⅛"
14-count	5⅝" x 5⅝"
18-count	4⅜" x 4⅜"
22-count	3⅝" x 3⅝"

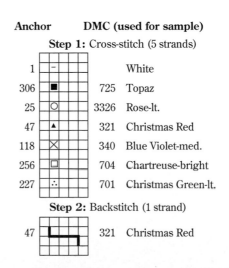

Anchor		DMC (used for sample)	
Step 1: Cross-stitch (5 strands)			
1	−		White
306	■	725	Topaz
25	O	3326	Rose-lt.
47	▲	321	Christmas Red
118	✕	340	Blue Violet-med.
256	☐	704	Chartreuse-bright
227	∴	701	Christmas Green-lt.
Step 2: Backstitch (1 strand)			
47		321	Christmas Red

Love Week

Stitch this elegant table runner for a wedding reception or silver anniversary,

or simply to express your feelings for your own lovey-dovey.

Love Bird Table Runner

SAMPLE
Stitched on white 32-count Belfast Linen over 2 threads, the finished design size is 6" x 5¾". The fabric was cut 28" x 58". With design centered horizontally, begin stitching bottom of design 10" from end of fabric. Stitch design at each end of runner. See Suppliers, page 144, for silk ribbon.

FABRICS	DESIGN SIZES
11-count	8⅝" x 8⅜"
14-count	6¾" x 6⅝"
18-count	5¼" x 5⅛"
22-count	4⅜" x 4⅛"

MATERIALS
Completed cross-stitch on white 32-count Belfast Linen; matching thread
1 (15" x 48½") piece white flannel
15 yards 4-mm dark green silk ribbon; matching thread
15 yards 4-mm light green silk ribbon; matching thread

3½ yards ¼"-wide white lace trim
5" square cardboard
Dressmaker's pen

DIRECTIONS
All seam allowances are ¼".
Note: Substitute ⅛"-wide satin or grosgrain ribbon for 4-mm silk ribbon if desired.
1. With designs centered horizontally and bottom of each design 5¼" from 1 end, trim design piece to 24½" x 48½". Zigzag-stitch along all raw edges. Center and baste flannel to wrong side of design piece.
2. With right sides facing and raw edges aligned, fold design piece in half lengthwise; stitch long edges together. Trim seam, center, and press seam open.
3. Referring to Diagram and using dressmaker's pen, measure and mark 3" from each end along sides. Draw line from

each mark to center seam at ends. Stitch along these lines, leaving an opening at 1 end for turning. Trim excess fabric and turn. Slipstitch opening closed.

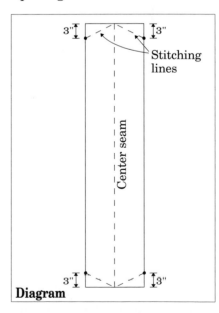

Diagram

4. From dark green ribbon and lace, cut 4 (13½") lengths and 4 (16") lengths each. From

light green ribbon, cut 2 (13½")
lengths and 2 (16") lengths.
Referring to photo, handstitch
2 (13½") dark green ribbons
and 1 (13½") light green
ribbon at 1 end of runner,
beginning 1" above design
and spacing ribbons 1" apart.
Slightly overlap each dark
green ribbon with 1 (13½")
length of lace; stitch in place.
Handstitch ends of ribbons to
back of runner. Referring to
photo, repeat with 2 (16")
lengths each of dark green
ribbon and lace and 1 (16")
length of light green ribbon
below design, following shape
of point. Repeat at other end
of runner.

5. Referring to Diagrams on
page 136 and using cardboard,
make 2 (5"-long) tassels from
remaining ribbon. Tack tassels
to points of runner.

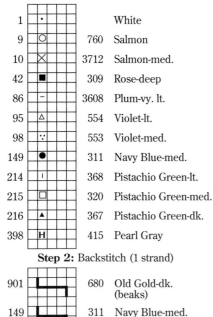

Anchor		DMC	(used for sample)

Step 1: Cross-stitch (2 strands)

1	·		White
9	O	760	Salmon
10	X	3712	Salmon-med.
42	■	309	Rose-deep
86	–	3608	Plum-vy. lt.
95	△	554	Violet-lt.
98	∴	553	Violet-med.
149	●	311	Navy Blue-med.
214	I	368	Pistachio Green-lt.
215	□	320	Pistachio Green-med.
216	▲	367	Pistachio Green-dk.
398	H	415	Pearl Gray

Step 2: Backstitch (1 strand)

901		680	Old Gold-dk. (beaks)
149		311	Navy Blue-med. (all else)

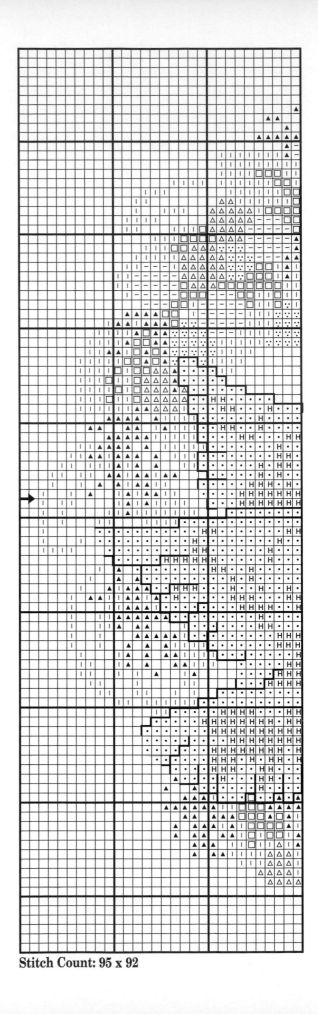

Stitch Count: 95 x 92

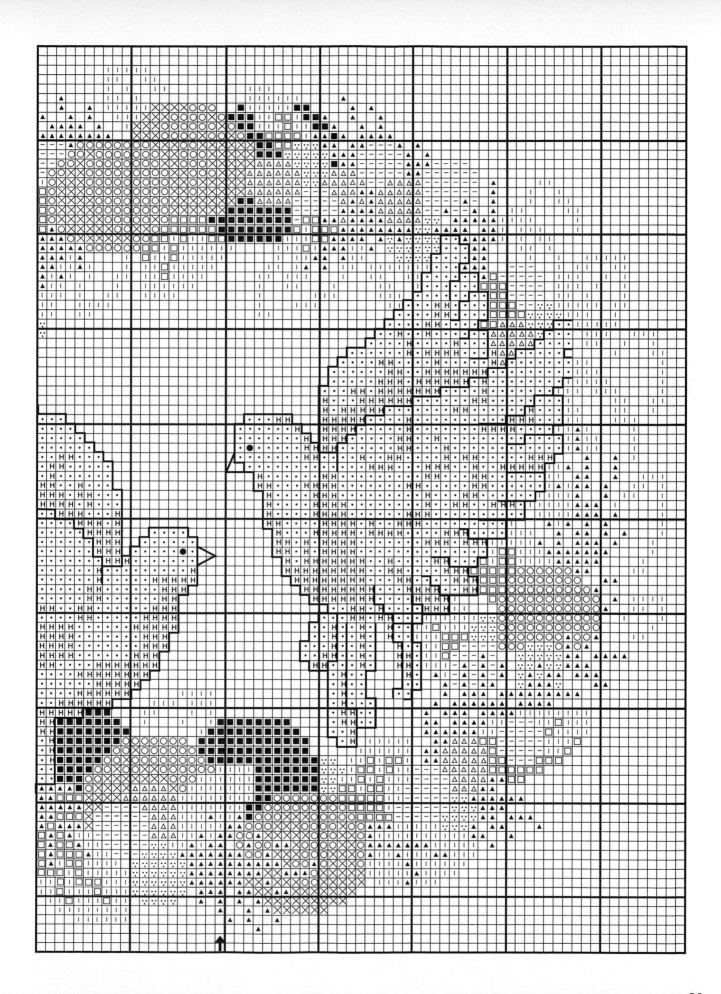

Valentine's Day

Let a floral heart convey your sweetest sentiments.
The nostalgic colors in this piece are reminiscent of the
charming vintage fabrics and fashions of the 1930s.

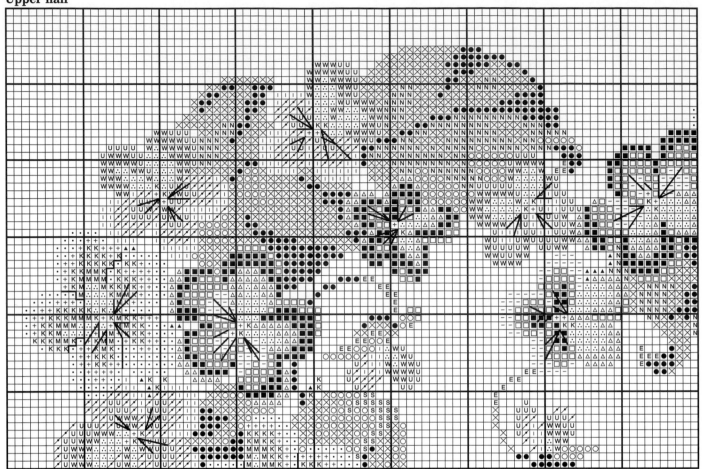

Heart of Pansies

SAMPLE
Stitched on antique tan 28-count Linen over 2 threads, the finished design size is 12" x 10⅜". The fabric was cut 18" x 17".

FABRICS	DESIGN SIZES
11-count	15¼" x 13¼"
14-count	12" x 10⅜"
18-count	9⅜" x 8⅛"
22-count	7⅝" x 6⅝"

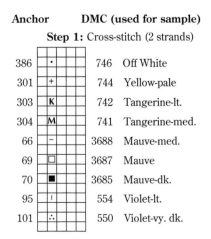

Anchor		DMC (used for sample)	
		Step 1: Cross-stitch (2 strands)	
386	·	746	Off White
301	+	744	Yellow-pale
303	K	742	Tangerine-lt.
304	M	741	Tangerine-med.
66	−	3688	Mauve-med.
69	□	3687	Mauve
70	■	3685	Mauve-dk.
95	I	554	Violet-lt.
101	∴	550	Violet-vy. dk.

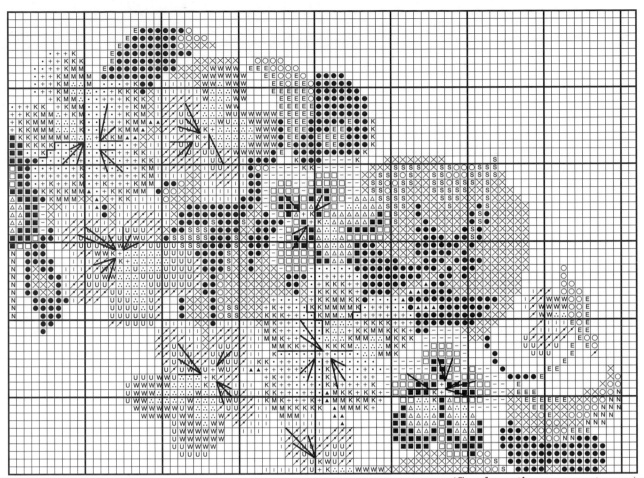

(Graph continues on next page.)

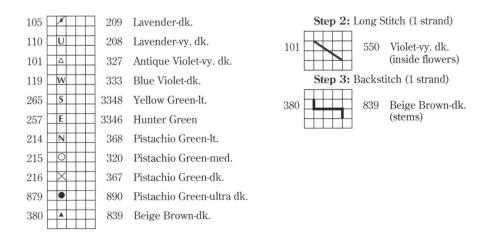

105	✁	209	Lavender-dk.
110	U	208	Lavender-vy. dk.
101	△	327	Antique Violet-vy. dk.
119	W	333	Blue Violet-dk.
265	S	3348	Yellow Green-lt.
257	E	3346	Hunter Green
214	N	368	Pistachio Green-lt.
215	O	320	Pistachio Green-med.
216	✕	367	Pistachio Green-dk.
879	●	890	Pistachio Green-ultra dk.
380	▲	839	Beige Brown-dk.

Step 2: Long Stitch (1 strand)

101   550   Violet-vy. dk.
(inside flowers)

Step 3: Backstitch (1 strand)

380   839   Beige Brown-dk.
(stems)

Lower half

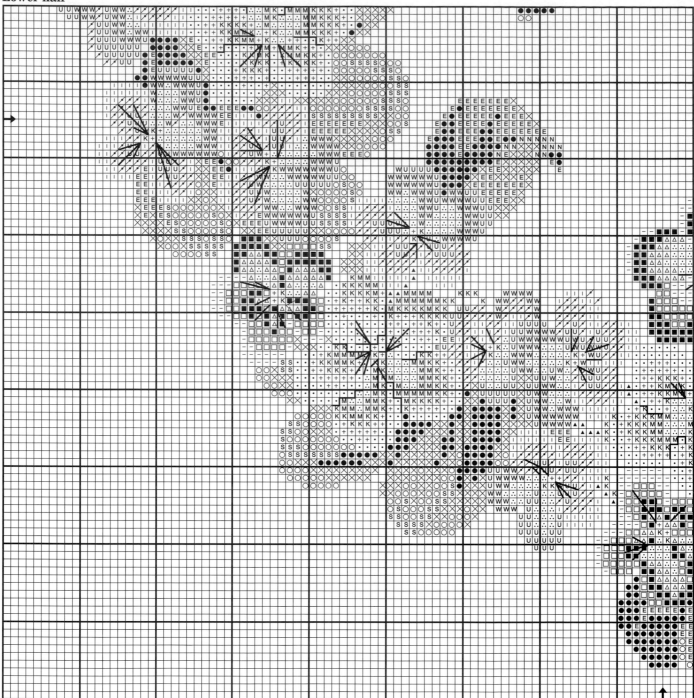

Stitch Count: 168 x 146

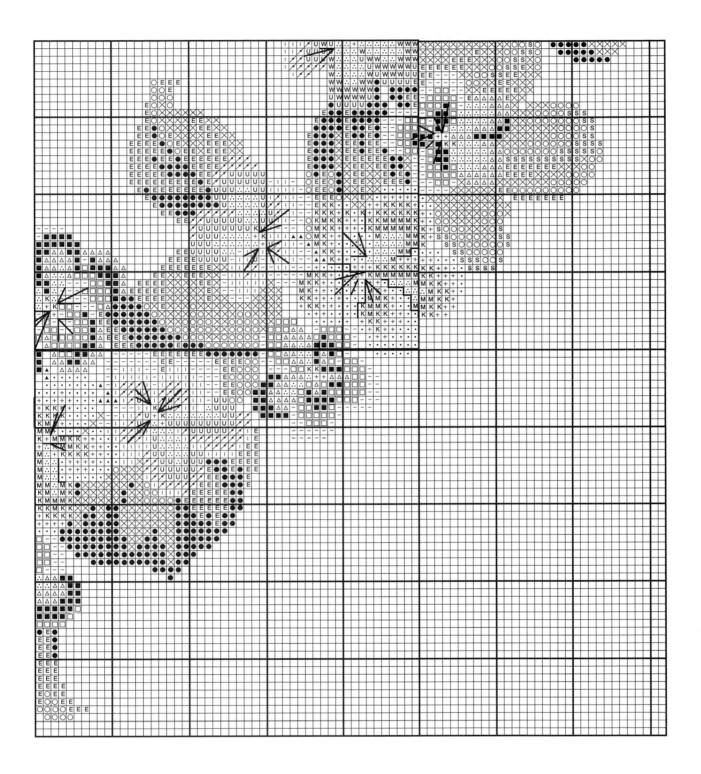

MARCH 17

St. Patrick's Day

Silk ribbon, glass beads, and embroidery floss in shades of cool green add textural interest to this beautiful piece. It is an affirmation of our need to believe in childhood dreams.

I Believe

SAMPLE
Stitched on antique white 28-count Cashel Linen over 2 threads, the finished design size is 7" x 12⅛". The fabric was cut 13" x 19". For bows, draw ribbon up through fabric and knot where indicated on graph. For woven ribbon heart, see Directions and Diagram. See pages 138 and 139 for special stitches. See Suppliers, page 144, for silk ribbon and Mill Hill seed beads. See Framing Ideas, page 140.

FABRICS	DESIGN SIZES
11-count	8⅞" x 15⅜"
14-count	7" x 12⅛"
18-count	5½" x 9⅜"
22-count	4½" x 7⅝"

MATERIALS
Completed cross-stitch on antique white 28-count Cashel Linen
⅞ yard 4-mm light green silk ribbon
⅞ yard 4-mm medium green silk ribbon
Embroidery needle
Fabric glue (optional)
Dressmaker's pen

DIRECTIONS
1. Referring to graph and using dressmaker's pen, transfer placement lines for woven ribbon heart to design piece.

2. From light green ribbon, cut 11 (2½") lengths. From medium green ribbon, cut 10 (2½") lengths.

3. Referring to Diagram and using embroidery needle, weave ribbons for heart, using light green for horizontal weave and medium green for vertical weave. If desired, secure ends of woven ribbons on back of design piece with small drops of fabric glue.

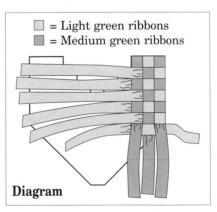

◻ = Light green ribbons
▨ = Medium green ribbons

Diagram

38

Stitch Count: 98 x 169

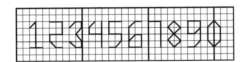

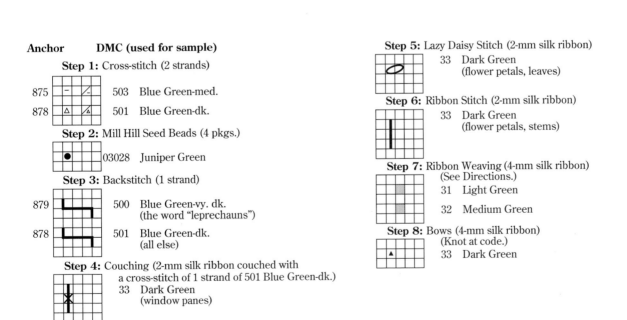

Anchor   **DMC (used for sample)**

Step 1: Cross-stitch (2 strands)

| 875 | 503 | Blue Green-med. |
| 878 | 501 | Blue Green-dk. |

Step 2: Mill Hill Seed Beads (4 pkgs.)

| | 03028 | Juniper Green |

Step 3: Backstitch (1 strand)

| 879 | 500 | Blue Green-vy. dk. (the word "leprechauns") |
| 878 | 501 | Blue Green-dk. (all else) |

Step 4: Couching (2-mm silk ribbon couched with a cross-stitch of 1 strand of 501 Blue Green-dk.)

| | 33 | Dark Green (window panes) |

Step 5: Lazy Daisy Stitch (2-mm silk ribbon)

| | 33 | Dark Green (flower petals, leaves) |

Step 6: Ribbon Stitch (2-mm silk ribbon)

| | 33 | Dark Green (flower petals, stems) |

Step 7: Ribbon Weaving (4-mm silk ribbon) (See Directions.)

| | 31 | Light Green |
| | 32 | Medium Green |

Step 8: Bows (4-mm silk ribbon) (Knot at code.)

| | 33 | Dark Green |

Vernal Equinox

Mark the beginning of spring with a lively collection of ribbon pansies, delphiniums, and geraniums abloom in colorful cross-stitched pots.

Stitch a Garden

SAMPLE
Stitched on dirty linen
25-count Dublin Linen over
2 threads, the finished design
size for flowerpots is 15⅝" x
2¾" (including repeat). Repeat
first flowerpot only. The fabric
was cut 26" x 22". See Step 1
of Directions before stitching
fabric. See Framing Ideas,
page 140.

FABRICS	DESIGN SIZES
11-count	17⅞" x 3⅛"
14-count	14" x 2⅜"
18-count	10⅞" x 1⅞"
22-count	8⅞" x 1½"

MATERIALS
Completed cross-stitch on dirty
   linen 25-count Dublin Linen
1½ yards ⅝"-wide multicolored
   wire-edged ribbon for pansy
   petals
⅜ yard ⅝"-wide light purple
   silk ribbon for pansy petals
1⅓ yards ⅛"-wide yellow silk
   ribbon for pansy eyes and
   delphinium stamens
1⅛ yards 1⅛"-wide dark
   mauve silk ribbon for
   delphinium petals

⅞ yard 1⅛"-wide light mauve
   silk ribbon for delphinium
   petals
1⅛ yards 1⅛"-wide purple
   silk ribbon for delphinium
   petals
3⅛ yards ⅝"-wide rose wire-
   edged ribbon for geranium
   petals
½ yard ⅝"-wide light green
   wire-edged ribbon for pansy
   leaves
⅜ yard 1⅝"-wide light green
   wire-edged ribbon for
   delphinium and geranium
   leaves
6 yards ⅛"-wide green silk
   ribbon for stems
8" length 1¼"-wide yellow
   variegated wire-edged
   ribbon for butterfly
6" length ¾"-wide rose
   variegated wire-edged
   ribbon for butterfly
6" length ¼"-wide ecru silk
   ribbon for butterfly
Thread to match ribbons
Dressmaker's pen
Craft wire
Fabric glue
Large-eyed needle
3 butterfly charms (See
   Suppliers, page 144.)

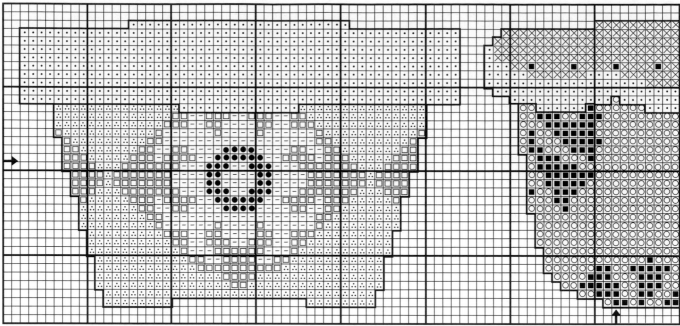

Stitch Count: 196 x 34 (for complete design)

DIRECTIONS

Note: For flower identification, refer to Placement Diagram on page 44.

1. Begin stitching left and bottom edges of flowerpot design each 5" from edge of fabric. Begin stitching quote with top left corner of quote 5½" from top edge of fabric and 11" from right edge of fabric.

2. To make petals for 1 pansy, cut 3 (3") lengths of multicolored ribbon and 1 (2½") length of light purple silk ribbon. Referring to Diagram 1, Figures A and B, mark curved line on each

ribbon. For each petal, run gathering thread along line; pull to gather tightly. Secure thread. Stitch 4 petals together along gathered edges.

3. To make eye for 1 pansy, cut 1 (3") length of ⅛"-wide yellow ribbon. Run gathering thread along 1 long edge; pull to gather tightly. Roll ribbon into tight circle. Tack eye to center of petals. Repeat steps 2 and 3 to make total of 5 pansies.

4. To make fallen pansy, cut, gather, and stitch together 2 (3") multicolored petals.

5. To make 1 delphinium flower, cut 1 (10") length of dark mauve ribbon. Fold ribbon in half lengthwise and press. Referring to Diagram 2, mark 6 lines 2" apart; then

draw curves connecting marks. Run gathering thread along curves; pull to gather tightly. Secure thread. Separate 2 layers to create double petals.

6. To make 1 stamen cluster, cut 1 (3") length of ⅛"-wide yellow ribbon. Beginning ¾" from 1 end, tie 3 knots in ribbon ¾" apart. Cut ribbon after each knot. Stitch stamens together ⅜" from knots. Trim excess ribbon. Tack cluster to center of 1 delphinium flower. Repeat steps 5 and 6 to make total of 11 delphinium flowers (4 dark mauve, 3 light mauve, and 4 purple).

7. To make 1 geranium flower, cut 1 (10") length of rose ribbon. Referring to Step 5, make flower, omitting reference to folding ribbon in half before forming flower. Repeat to make total of 11 geranium flowers.

8. To make 1 pansy leaf, follow directions for making pansy petals in Step 2, using 1 (3") length of ⅝"-wide light

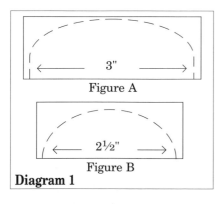

Figure A

Figure B

Diagram 1

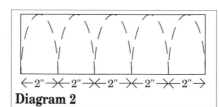

Diagram 2

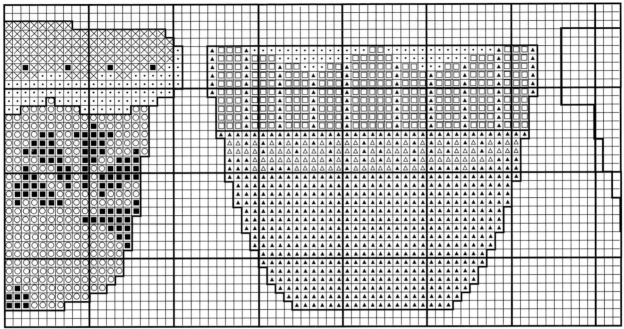

(Graph continues on next page.)

green ribbon. Repeat to make total of 5 leaves.

9. To make 1 delphinium leaf, cut 1 (7½") length of 1⅝"-wide light green ribbon. Fold ribbon in half lengthwise and press. Referring to Diagram 3, fold raw ends under ¼". Run gathering thread along folded edges; pull to gather moderately. Secure thread. Open leaf.

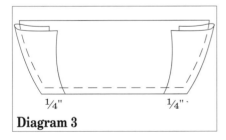

Diagram 3

10. To make 1 geranium leaf, follow directions for making pansy petals in Step 2, using 1 (3") length of 1⅝"-wide light green ribbon. Repeat to make total of 2 leaves.

11. To make stems, referring to Placement Diagram, cut

craft wire into desired lengths. Wrap wires with ⅛"-wide green ribbon, securing ends with glue.

12. To make ribbon butterfly, cut yellow and rose variegated ribbons each in half. Run gathering thread along 1 long edge of each ribbon. Pull to gather tightly. Secure thread. Stitch gathered edges of matching pieces together; open wings. Referring to photo, stack yellow wings on top of rose wings. Cut 2" length of ecru ribbon and wrap around center of butterfly; tack. Knot ends of remaining ecru ribbon and fold in half. Tack to back of butterfly for antennae (see photo).

13. Referring to photo and Placement Diagram, page 44, couch stems to design piece, using large-eyed needle and remaining ⅛"-wide green ribbon. (See page 138 for couching diagram.) Tack flowers and leaves to stems. Tack ribbon butterfly and charms to design piece. Frame as desired.

Anchor		DMC (used for sample)	

Step 1: Cross-stitch (2 strands)

Anchor		DMC	
366	–	951	Peach Pecan-lt.
969	·	316	Antique Mauve-med.
928	□	598	Turquoise-lt.
875	○	503	Blue Green-med.
373	●	422	Hazel Nut Brown-lt.
889	■	370	Mustard-med.
830	△	644	Beige Gray-med.
903	▲	640	Beige Gray-vy. dk.
397	✕	453	Shell Gray-lt.
400	∴	414	Steel Gray-dk.

Step 2: Backstitch (1 strand)

905		3781	Mocha Brown-dk.

Step 3: French Knot (1 strand)

905	●	3781	Mocha Brown-dk.

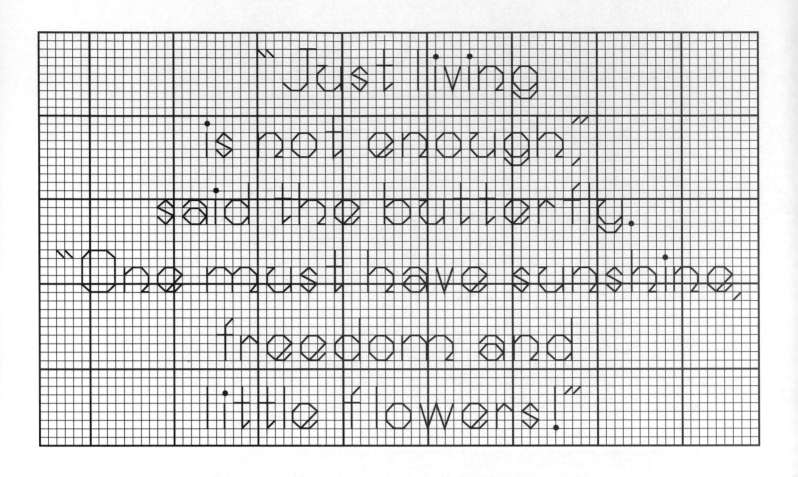

"Just living
is not enough"
said the butterfly.
"One must have sunshine,
freedom and
little flowers!"

BONUS STITCHES

The simple techniques for making ribbon flowers can be applied to a variety of projects: For a floral brooch, cut a piece of cardboard in the desired shape and size. Hot-glue flowers to cover the cardboard. Glue a pin back to the wrong side of the brooch. Or glue flowers to purchased button covers or to a barrette.

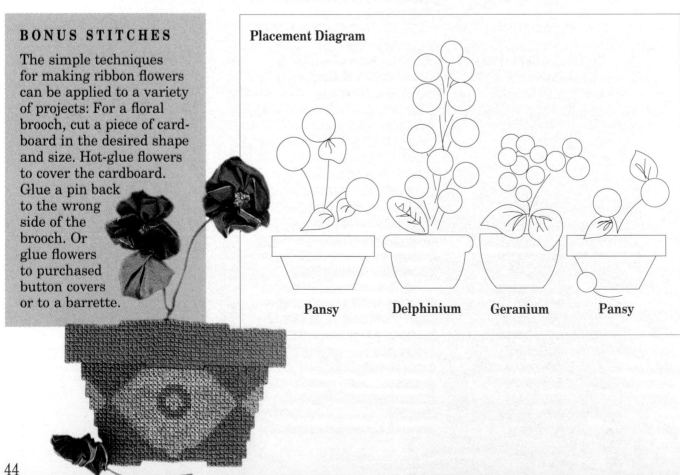

Placement Diagram

Pansy   Delphinium   Geranium   Pansy

Tulip Festival

When hundreds of acres of tulips bloom in Washington State's Skagit Valley, the residents host a flower-filled festival. Catch the spirit with this cross-stitched tulip design that brightens up a gingham gift stocking.

Tulip Stocking

SAMPLE
Stitched on cream 14-count Aida over 1 thread, the finished design size is 2½" x 2" for 1 repeat. The fabric was cut 10" x 6". See Step 2 of Directions before stitching. See Suppliers, page 144, for a stocking kit.

FABRICS	DESIGN SIZES
11-count	3⅛" x 2½"
18-count	2" x 1½"
22-count	1⅝" x 1¼"

MATERIALS
Completed cross-stitch on cream 14-count Aida
½ yard 45"-wide tulip print cotton fabric; matching thread
½ yard 45"-wide contrasting plaid fabric for lining
Dressmaker's pen
⅝ yard ⅜"-wide red grosgrain ribbon

DIRECTIONS
All seam allowances are ½".
1. Enlarge and transfer stocking pattern to tracing paper. Cut out. Transfer pattern to fabrics. Cut 2 from tulip print for stocking and 2 from contrasting plaid for lining.
2. Centering design vertically, begin stitching first motif 1½" from left edge of fabric. Repeat motif 3 times.
3. With design centered, trim design piece to 8¼" x 2¾". Zigzag-stitch all raw edges. Referring to photo, pin design piece to right side of 1 tulip print stocking piece, 3¼" below top edge.
4. From ribbon, cut 2 (8¼") lengths and 1 (4") length.

Stitch 1 (8¼") ribbon along each long edge of design piece, covering raw edges.
5. With right sides facing and raw edges aligned, stitch stocking front to back, catching design piece and ribbons in seam and leaving top edge open. Turn.
6. For hanger, fold 4" ribbon in half to make a loop. With raw edges aligned and loop toward center, baste hanger to right side of stocking back at top corner above heel.
7. To make lining, with right sides facing and raw edges aligned, stitch lining pieces together, leaving top edge open and large opening in side seam above heel. Clip curves but do not turn. With right sides facing, slide lining over stocking, matching side seams. With raw edges aligned, stitch along top edge of stocking, securing hanger in seam. Turn through opening in lining. Slipstitch opening closed. Tuck lining inside stocking.

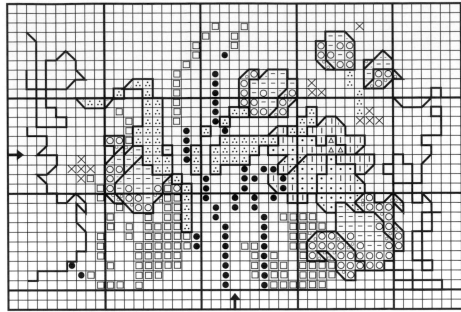

Stitch Count: 35 x 28 (for 1 repeat)

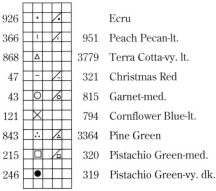

Anchor			DMC (used for sample)	
	Step 1:	Cross-stitch (2 strands)		
926	·	⟋	Ecru	
366	ı	⟋	951	Peach Pecan-lt.
868	△		3779	Terra Cotta-vy. lt.
47	–	⟋	321	Christmas Red
43	O	⟋	815	Garnet-med.
121	X		794	Cornflower Blue-lt.
843	∴	⟋	3364	Pine Green
215	□	⟋	320	Pistachio Green-med.
246	●		319	Pistachio Green-vy. dk.
	Step 2:	Backstitch (1 strand)		
147	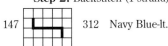		312	Navy Blue-lt.

BONUS STITCHES
For a seasonal gardening hat, repeat the motif to make a hatband. Or stitch the decorative border on a hand towel; then edge the design with ribbon to complement the towel.

Each square = 1". Pattern includes ½" seam allowance.

STOCKING

Cut 2 from tulip print.

For lining, cut 2 from
contrasting plaid.

Astronomy Week

Pay a visit to your local planetarium for a clear view of the heavens. Then make these bright little pillows to bring the sun and moon within easy reach.

Sun and Moon Pillows

SAMPLE for Sun Pillow
Stitched on cream 28-count
Cashel Linen over 2 threads,
the finished design size is
6⅜" x 6⅜". The fabric was cut
18" x 23".

FABRICS	DESIGN SIZES
11-count	8⅛" x 8⅛"
14-count	6⅜" x 6⅜"
18-count	5" x 5"
22-count	4" x 4⅛"

SAMPLE for Moon Pillow
Stitched on cream 28-count
Cashel Linen over 2 threads,
the finished design size is
5¼" x 5". The fabric was cut
16" x 20".

FABRICS	DESIGN SIZES
11-count	6¾" x 6⅜"
14-count	5¼" x 5"
18-count	4⅛" x 3⅞"
22-count	3⅜" x 3⅛"

MATERIALS (for both pillows)
Completed cross-stitch designs
   on cream 28-count Cashel
   Linen; matching thread
½ yard 45"-wide flannel
⅜ yard gold chintz fabric;
   matching thread
Polyester stuffing
3¾ yards 4-mm gold silk
   ribbon (See Suppliers,
   page 144.)
Large-eyed needle

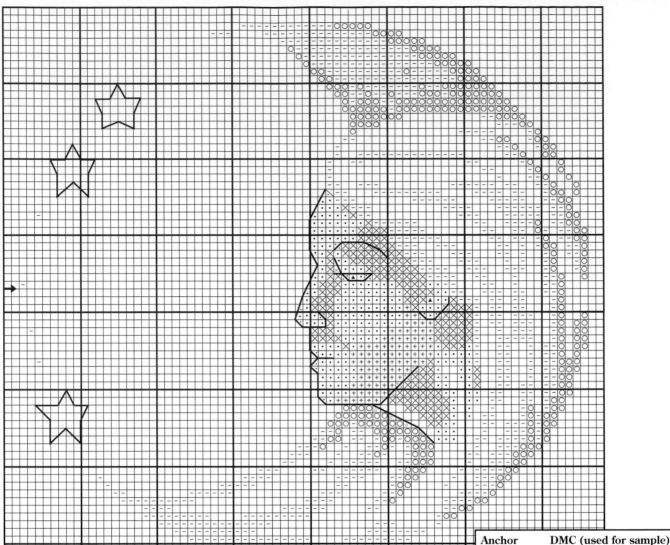

Stitch Count: 74 x 70

DIRECTIONS
All seam allowances are ¼".

1. With design centered, trim sun design piece to 16" x 18½" and moon design piece to 14" x 16½". From flannel, cut 1 piece each to these measurements. Aligning raw edges, baste flannel pieces to wrong side of matching design pieces.

2. On sun pillow, with right sides facing and raw edges aligned, stitch long edges of design piece together to make tube. Trim seam and turn. Center seam at back and press. Remove basting. Repeat for moon pillow.

3. From chintz, cut 2 (10") squares for sun pillow and 2

(8½") squares for moon pillow. With right sides facing and raw edges aligned, stitch 10" squares together, leaving an opening. Clip corners and turn. Stuff pillow moderately. Slipstitch opening closed. Repeat with 8½" squares.

4. Fold top edge of sun design piece ¼" to back. Fold bottom edge ¼" to front. Wrap sun design piece around its pillow, overlapping short edges to fit pillow snugly. Pin. Slide design piece off pillow. Slipstitch edges together. Slide design piece on pillow. Repeat for moon pillow.

5. From ribbon, cut 4 (16") lengths for each pillow. On sun

pillow, stitch 1 length through each adjacent edge of design piece at center (see photo). Tie ribbons into bows. Repeat for moon pillow.

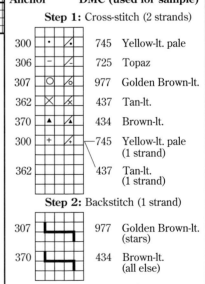

Anchor			DMC (used for sample)	
Step 1: Cross-stitch (2 strands)				
300	·	⁄	745	Yellow-lt. pale
306	−	⁄	725	Topaz
307	O	⁄	977	Golden Brown-lt.
362	×	⁄	437	Tan-lt.
370	▲	⁄	434	Brown-lt.
300	+	⁄	745	Yellow-lt. pale (1 strand)
362			437	Tan-lt. (1 strand)
Step 2: Backstitch (1 strand)				
307			977	Golden Brown-lt. (stars)
370			434	Brown-lt. (all else)

Stitch Count: 89 x 90

Anchor			DMC	(used for sample)
Step 1: Cross-stitch (2 strands)				
306	–	/	725	Topaz
307	O	⊘	977	Golden Brown-lt.
362	X	⊠	437	Tan-lt.
370	▲	◢	434	Brown-lt.
Step 2: Backstitch (1 strand)				
370			434	Brown-lt.

APRIL 15
Strawberry Hill Race

The tailgate picnics at the Strawberry Hill steeplechase in Richmond, Virginia, are as eagerly anticipated as the race itself. This pretty berries-and-cream table-cloth is perfect for the occasion—or an intimate supper at home.

52

Strawberry Tablecloth

SAMPLE
Stitched on rose/cream 28-count Silvretta over 2 threads, the finished design size for 1 motif is 2¾" x 2¾". The fabric was cut 54" x 54". See Placement Diagram before stitching. See Suppliers, page 144, for Silvretta fabric.

FABRICS	DESIGN SIZES
11-count	3½" x 3½"
14-count	2¾" x 2¾"
18-count	2⅛" x 2⅛"
22-count	1¾" x 1¾"

MATERIALS
Completed cross-stitch on rose/cream 28-count Silvretta; matching thread

DIRECTIONS
1. Trim design piece to 51" x 51", following rose lines in fabric. Zigzag-stitch raw edges.

2. Turn zigzagged edges under ¼" and press. Then turn edges under 1½" (see Placement Diagram), mitering corners. Press. Slipstitch edges to secure.

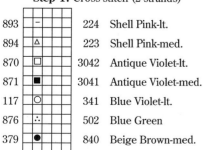

Anchor		DMC (used for sample)	
\multicolumn{4}{Step 1: Cross-stitch (2 strands)}			
893	–	224	Shell Pink-lt.
894	△	223	Shell Pink-med.
870	□	3042	Antique Violet-lt.
871	■	3041	Antique Violet-med.
117	○	341	Blue Violet-lt.
876	∴	502	Blue Green
379	●	840	Beige Brown-med.

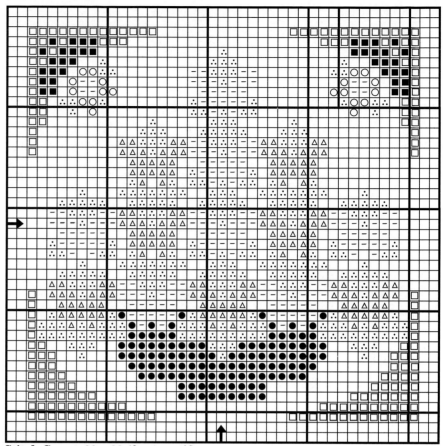

Stitch Count: 39 x 39 (for 1 motif)

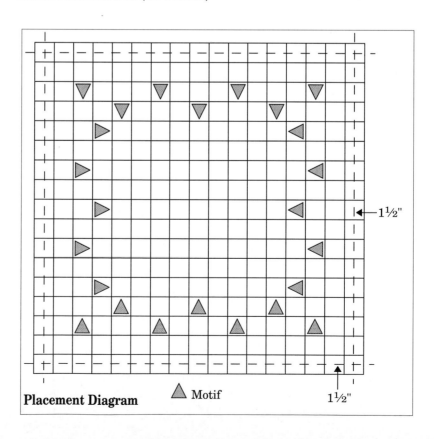

Placement Diagram   △ Motif   1½"

APRIL 16

Easter

Celebrate Easter with two delights to cross-stitch. The elegant vanity tray,

at right, provides a year-round breath of spring, while the cheerful sampler,

shown on page 58, beams with seasonal whimsy.

Floral Vanity Tray

SAMPLE
Stitched on cream 32-count
Belfast Linen over 2 threads,
the finished design size is 10" x
6". The fabric was cut 16" x 12".

FABRICS	DESIGN SIZES
11-count	14½" x 8¾"
14-count	11⅜" x 6⅞"
18-count	8⅞" x 5⅜"
22-count	7¼" x 4⅜"

MATERIALS
Completed cross-stitch on
    cream 32-count Belfast
    Linen; matching thread
6¾" x 10¾" piece of mat board
Wooden frame with 6½" x 10½"
    front opening and glass
2 wooden handles with screws
Wood stain or acrylic paint in
    desired color
6¾" x 10¾" piece of balsa
    wood or sturdy cardboard
Small tacks
8 adhesive felt dots

DIRECTIONS
Note: Frame will have to be
custom-made because of its
unique size.

   1. Zigzag-stitch along raw
edges of design piece. Lace
design piece to mat board (see
Framing Ideas, page 140).

   2. Stain or paint frame and
handles as desired. Let dry.
Center and screw handles onto
short sides of frame. Insert
glass, design piece, and then
balsa wood into frame. Secure
back with small tacks.

   3. Apply adhesive felt dots
to corners and sides of frame
on back.

Anchor		DMC (used for sample)	
Step 1: Cross-stitch (2 strands)			
892	B	3770	Peach Pecan-vy. lt.
933	U	3774	Peach Pecan-med.
868	S	3779	Terra Cotta-vy. lt.
8	– /	760	Salmon
9	O	352	Coral-lt.
10	G	351	Coral
11	·	3328	Salmon-dk.
13	X	347	Salmon-vy. dk.

		DMC	
25	M	3326	Rose-lt.
969	■ /	3727	Antique Mauve-lt.
869	K	3743	Antique Violet-vy. lt.
95	□ /	554	Violet-lt.
98	+	553	Violet-med.
343	H	3753	Antique Blue-ultra vy. lt. (1 strand)
920	E	932	Antique Blue-lt. (1 strand)
921	∴ /	931	Antique Blue-med. (1 strand)
779	●	926	Slate Green (1 strand)
242	△ /	989	Forest Green
258	▲	904	Parrot Green-vy. dk.
212	▽ /	561	Jade-vy. dk.
378	/	841	Beige Brown-lt. (1 strand)
378	I	841	Beige Brown-lt.
309	N /	435	Brown-vy. lt.
371	▣	433	Brown-med.

Step 2: Backstitch (1 strand)

22		816	Garnet (coral flowers)
970		315	Antique Mauve-vy. dk. (cream flowers)
371		433	Brown-med. (basket)

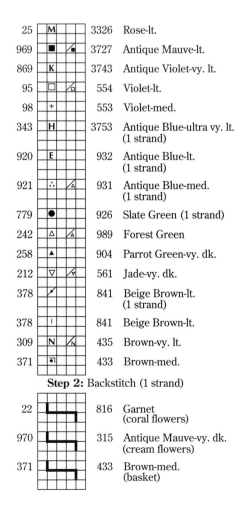

Graph begins on page 56.

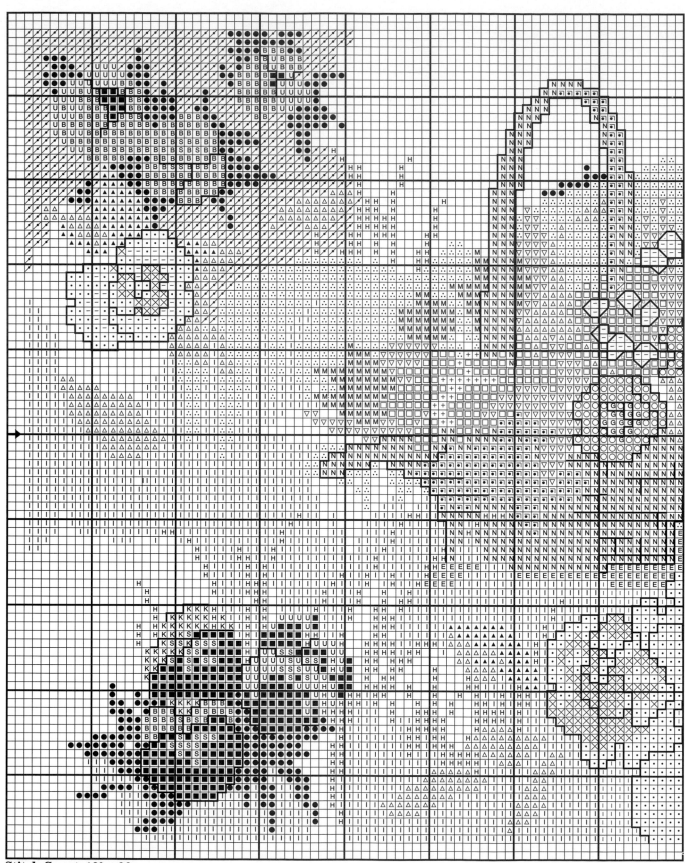

Stitch Count: 160 x 96

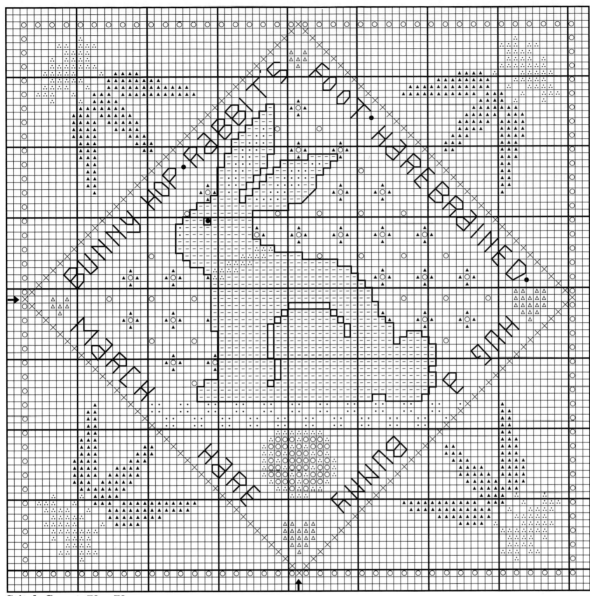

Stitch Count: 79 x 79

Bunny Sampler

SAMPLE

Stitched on yellow 14-count Aida over 1 thread, the finished design size is 5⅝" x 5⅝". The fabric was cut 12" x 12". See Framing Ideas, page 140.

FABRICS	DESIGN SIZES
11-count	7⅛" x 7⅛"
18-count	4⅜" x 4⅜"
22-count	3⅝" x 3⅝"

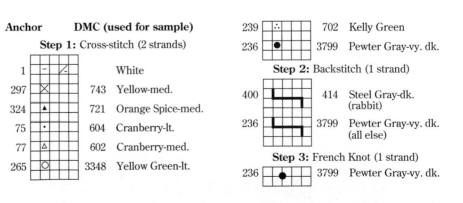

Anchor		DMC (used for sample)	
Step 1: Cross-stitch (2 strands)			
1	– ⁄		White
297	✕	743	Yellow-med.
324	▲	721	Orange Spice-med.
75	•	604	Cranberry-lt.
77	△	602	Cranberry-med.
265	○	3348	Yellow Green-lt.
239	∴	702	Kelly Green
236	●	3799	Pewter Gray-vy. dk.

Step 2: Backstitch (1 strand)

400		414	Steel Gray-dk. (rabbit)
236		3799	Pewter Gray-vy. dk. (all else)

Step 3: French Knot (1 strand)

236	●	3799	Pewter Gray-vy. dk.

59

MAY 14
Mother's Day

Give bunches of flowers to Mom on her special day. Here are two everlasting bouquets she'll adore: a duplicate-stitched sweater, *at left,* for cool spring days and elegant beaded sachets, *page 62,* to surround her with fragrant luxury.

Roses and Lilacs Sweater

SAMPLE
Stitched on purchased cotton sweater with a gauge of 7½ stitches per 1", the finished design size is 1⅝" x 1½" for 1 sleeve repeat and 4½" x 4⅝" for 1 waist repeat. With center of sleeve repeat on sleeve crease, begin stitching bottom of design ⅜" above ribbing. Stitch around sleeve to fill. With design centered on front of sweater, begin stitching waist repeat with bottom of design ⅜" above ribbing. Stitch to each side seam. Repeat for back of sweater. See page 138 for duplicate-stitch diagrams and Suppliers, page 144, for Paternayan Persian yarn.

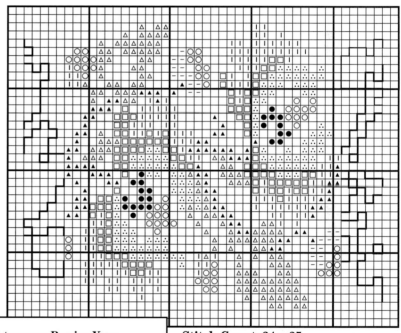

Stitch Count: 34 x 35
(for 1 waist repeat)

Paternayan Persian Yarn
(used for sample)

Step 1: Duplicate stitch (1 strand)

·	907 American Beauty-ultra vy. lt.
–	905 American Beauty-lt.
○	903 American Beauty-med.
∴	333 Lavender-lt.
●	311 Grape-dk.
I	322 Plum-med.
□	321 Plum-dk.
△	643 Khaki Green
▲	641 Khaki Green-dk.

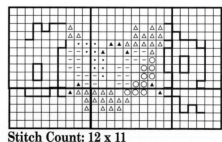

Stitch Count: 12 x 11
(for 1 sleeve repeat)

Beaded Sachets

SAMPLE for Designs 1 and 2
Stitched on moss green 27-count Linda over 2 threads, the finished design size for each is 3⅝" x 3⅝". The fabric was cut 8" x 8" for each. See Suppliers, page 144, for Anchor Marlitt floss and Mill Hill seed beads. See page 137 for beadwork diagrams. An alternative fabric suitable for this design is 14-count; the finished design size is 3½" x 3½".

MATERIALS (for 1 sachet)
Completed cross-stitch on moss green 27-count Linda; matching thread
⅛ yard unstitched moss green 27-count Linda
Fusible interfacing
Mill Hill seed beads: 3 packages of #02009 Ice Lilac, 1 package of #02006 Ice Blue
Beading needle
Potpourri

DIRECTIONS
All seam allowances are ¼".
1. With design centered, trim design piece to 4" x 4". From unstitched Linda, cut 4" square for back. Zigzag-stitch all raw edges.
2. From interfacing, cut 2 (4") squares. Following manufacturer's directions, fuse 1 interfacing square each to wrong side of design piece and back.
3. With right sides facing and raw edges aligned, stitch design piece to back, leaving 2" opening. Clip corners and turn.
4. To make beaded edging, thread beading needle with doubled length of thread. Bring needle up through sachet front, ¹⁄₁₆" from edge of stitched design.

Referring to Diagram, stitch beaded edging around sachet, using 10 ice lilac beads, 3 ice blue beads, and then 10 more ice lilac beads for each loop.

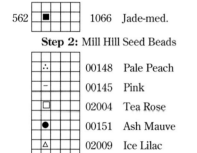

Diagram

5. Stuff sachet firmly with potpourri. Slipstitch opening closed.

Design 1

DMC		Marlitt (used for sample)	

Step 1: Cross-stitch (2 strands)

562	■	1066	Jade-med.

Step 2: Mill Hill Seed Beads

	∴	00148	Pale Peach
	–	00145	Pink
	□	02004	Tea Rose
	●	00151	Ash Mauve
	△	02009	Ice Lilac
	○	02006	Ice Blue
	✕	00561	Ice Green

Design 2

DMC		Marlitt (used for sample)	

Step 1: Cross-stitch (2 strands)

3326	I	830	Rose-lt.
562	■	1066	Jade-med.

Step 2: Mill Hill Seed Beads

	∴	00148	Pale Peach
	–	00145	Pink
	□	02004	Tea Rose
	●	00151	Ash Mauve
	△	02009	Ice Lilac
	○	02006	Ice Blue
	✕	00561	Ice Green

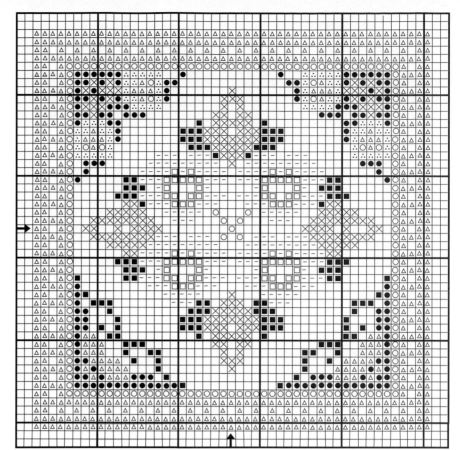

Stitch Count: 49 x 49 (Design 1)

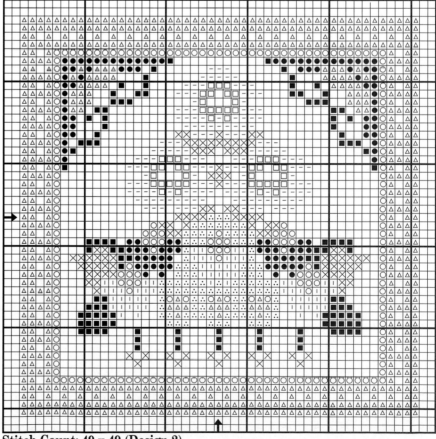

Stitch Count: 49 x 49 (Design 2)

Dolley Madison's Birthday

As First Lady, Dolley Madison was renowned as the nation's premier party-giver. Your favorite hostess will treasure this elegant serving tray, *at left,* or the ribbon-embellished teacup, *page 66,* as a gesture of thanks for her hospitality.

Tea Tray for Two

SAMPLE
Stitched on antique white 32-count Belfast Linen over 2 threads, the finished design size for 1 repeat is 2¼" x 4¾". The fabric was cut 16" x 12". Center and stitch repeat to fill, leaving 3" of unstitched fabric at each end. See pages 138 and 139 for special stitches.

FABRICS	DESIGN SIZES
11-count	3⅛" x 6⅞"
14-count	2½" x 5½"
18-count	2" x 4¼"
22-count	1⅝" x 3½"

MATERIALS
Completed cross-stitch on antique white 32-count Belfast Linen
6¼" x 10" piece mat board
Wooden frame with 6" x 9¾" opening and glass
Forest green acrylic paint
Paintbrush
Sandpaper (optional)
2 brass handles with screws
6¼" x 10" piece balsa wood
Small tacks
Hot-glue gun and glue sticks
Felt to match outside dimensions of frame

DIRECTIONS
Note: Frame will have to be custom-made because of its unique size.

1. Zigzag-stitch along raw edges of design piece; lace to mat board (see Framing Ideas, page 140).

2. Paint frame; let dry. If desired, sand frame for an aged effect. Center and screw handles onto short sides of frame. Insert glass, design piece, and then balsa wood into frame. Secure back with small tacks.

3. Hot-glue felt piece to bottom of tray, aligning edges.

Just Your Cup of Tea

SAMPLE
Stitched on white 32-count
Belfast Linen over 2 threads,
the finished design size is
2" x 1⅜". The fabric was cut
8" x 8". See Suppliers, page
144, for spoon charm. See
Framing Ideas, page 140.

FABRICS
11-count
14-count
18-count
22-count

DESIGN SIZES
3" x 2"
2⅜" x 1⅝"
1⅞" x 1¼"
1½" x 1"

MATERIALS
Completed cross-stitch on
  white 32-count Belfast Linen
1 yard each 4-mm silk ribbon:
  light mauve, medium mauve,
  dark mauve, lavender, pale
  yellow, light green, medium
  green

DIRECTIONS
  1. Referring to photo,
Placement Diagram, and stitch
diagrams on pages 137–139,
stitch following ribbon embell-
ishments: For rosettes, cut 1
(6") length each of medium and

dark mauve ribbon. Run gathering thread along 1 long edge
of each ribbon; pull to gather
tightly. Roll each into rosette,
tacking ribbon to secure. Stitch
rosettes to design piece where
indicated.
  2. For forget-me-nots, make
French knots using lavender
ribbon. For forget-me-not cen-
ters, make French knots using
pale yellow ribbon. For rosebuds, make long stitches using
mauve ribbons. For leaves,
make long stitches using green
ribbons.
  3. Frame as desired.

Tea Tray for Two

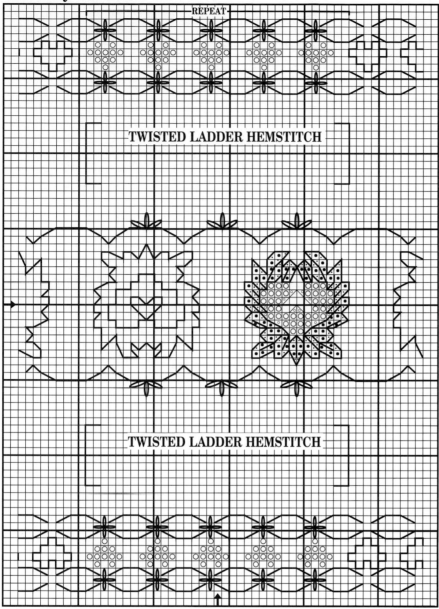

TWISTED LADDER HEMSTITCH

TWISTED LADDER HEMSTITCH

REPEAT

Stitch Count: 35 x 76 (for 1 repeat)

Tea Tray for Two

Anchor		DMC (used for sample)	

Step 1: Cross-stitch (2 strands)

| 969 | 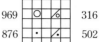 | 316 | Antique Mauve-med. |
| 876 | | 502 | Blue Green |

Step 2: Backstitch (1 strand)

| 969 | | 316 | Antique Mauve-med. (hearts) |
| 879 | | 500 | Blue Green-vy. dk. (all else) |

Step 3: Lazy Daisy (1 strand)

| 879 | | 500 | Blue Green-vy. dk. |

Step 4: Twisted Ladder Hemstitch

| 969 | | 316 | Antique Mauve-med. Remove 16 horizontal threads. Hemstitch top and bottom edges in groups of 4 vertical threads; then work twist. |

Just Your Cup of Tea

Anchor		DMC (used for sample)	

Step 1: Cross-stitch (2 strands)

| 968 | | 778 | Antique Mauve-vy. lt. |
| 969 | | 316 | Antique Mauve-med. |

Just Your Cup of Tea

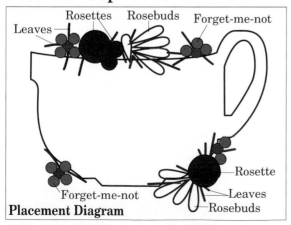

Rosettes   Rosebuds   Forget-me-not

Leaves

Forget-me-not   Rosette

Leaves

Rosebuds

Placement Diagram

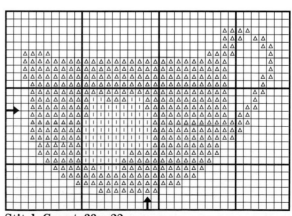

Stitch Count: 33 x 22

National Rose Month

Capture the essence of our national flower in this lavish cross-stitched design. The Victorian-inspired pillow combines the vibrant colors of rose petals with rich fabrics and trims.

Rose Garden Pillow

SAMPLE
Stitched on black 32-count Belfast Linen over 2 threads, the finished design size is 13⅝" x 5½" (including repeat). The fabric was cut 18" x 10". Centering the design vertically, begin stitching first motif 2½" from left edge of fabric. Refer to the Placement Diagram before stitching.

FABRICS	DESIGN SIZES
11-count	19⅞" x 8⅛"
14-count	15⅝" x 6⅜"
18-count	12⅛" x 5"
22-count	10" x 4"

MATERIALS
Completed cross-stitch on black 32-count Belfast Linen; matching thread
⅓ yard unstitched black 32-count Belfast Linen
1 yard ⅛"-wide burgundy upholstery cording; matching thread
1 skein #814 burgundy DMC Pearl Cotton, size 3
2½" square cardboard
½ yard 45"-wide burgundy crushed velvet
½ yard metallic-accented striped fabric
14⅝" x 9½" piece black velvet
⅞ yard 1"-wide black upholstery trim with tassels
Dressmaker's chalk pencil
Polyester stuffing

DIRECTIONS
All seam allowances are ¼".

1. Using chalk pencil, center and transfer valance stitching line to design piece. Trim design ¼" outside stitching line and to within ½" of each short end and top. Using design piece as pattern, cut matching piece from unstitched Belfast Linen for valance backing. With right sides facing and raw edges aligned, stitch backing to design piece, leaving top edge open. Turn.

2. Referring to photo, tack burgundy cording along curved edge of valance. Referring to Diagrams on page 136 and using cardboard square and pearl cotton, make 3 (2½") tassels. Tack 1 tassel to bottom point of each valance section.

3. For pillow front: From crushed velvet, cut 2 (3" x 30") strips. From striped fabric, cut 2 (3¼" x 14⅝") strips, following stripes.

4. Run gathering threads along each long edge of crushed velvet strips; pull to gather strips to equal 14⅝". Secure threads. With right sides facing and raw edges aligned, stitch 1 gathered velvet strip and 1 striped strip together along 1 long edge. Repeat with remaining crushed velvet and striped strips. Set aside.

5. With right sides up, align top edge of valance with 1 long edge of black velvet piece. Baste together along top edge. With right sides facing and raw edges aligned, stitch 1 joined crushed velvet/striped piece to top edge of valance along long edge of crushed velvet strip. Repeat to stitch remaining crushed velvet/striped piece to bottom edge of black velvet piece.

6. For pillow back, cut 1 (14⅝" x 20") piece from remaining crushed velvet. With right sides facing and raw edges aligned, stitch pillow back to pillow front, catching short ends of valance in seam and leaving an opening for turning. Turn. Stuff moderately. Slipstitch opening closed.

7. From upholstery trim, cut 2 (14⅛") lengths. Turn under raw ends and tack 1 length to each short edge of pillow.

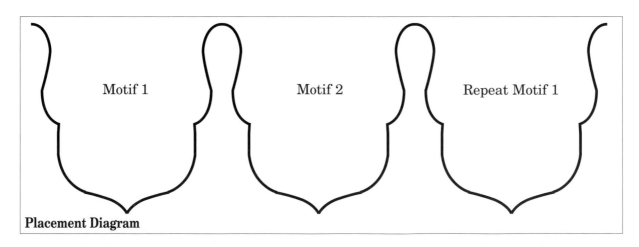

Motif 1   Motif 2   Repeat Motif 1

Placement Diagram

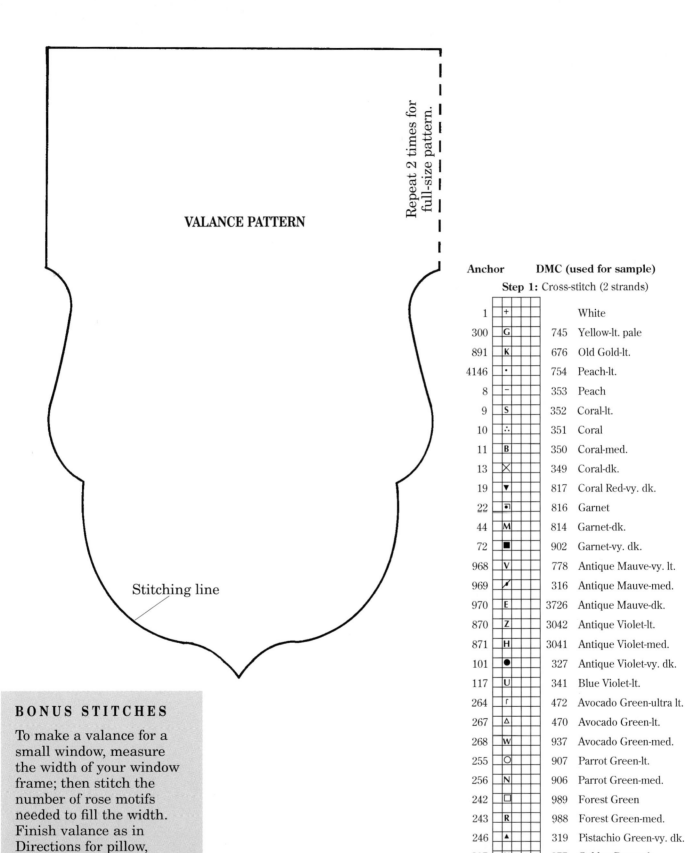

VALANCE PATTERN

Repeat 2 times for full-size pattern.

Stitching line

BONUS STITCHES

To make a valance for a small window, measure the width of your window frame; then stitch the number of rose motifs needed to fill the width. Finish valance as in Directions for pillow, adding a casing to the top back for hanging.

Anchor		DMC (used for sample)	
	Step 1: Cross-stitch (2 strands)		
1	+		White
300	G	745	Yellow-lt. pale
891	K	676	Old Gold-lt.
4146	·	754	Peach-lt.
8	–	353	Peach
9	S	352	Coral-lt.
10	∴	351	Coral
11	B	350	Coral-med.
13	✕	349	Coral-dk.
19	▼	817	Coral Red-vy. dk.
22	◙	816	Garnet
44	M	814	Garnet-dk.
72	■	902	Garnet-vy. dk.
968	V	778	Antique Mauve-vy. lt.
969	◢	316	Antique Mauve-med.
970	E	3726	Antique Mauve-dk.
870	Z	3042	Antique Violet-lt.
871	H	3041	Antique Violet-med.
101	●	327	Antique Violet-vy. dk.
117	U	341	Blue Violet-lt.
264	⌐	472	Avocado Green-ultra lt.
267	△	470	Avocado Green-lt.
268	W	937	Avocado Green-med.
255	O	907	Parrot Green-lt.
256	N	906	Parrot Green-med.
242	☐	989	Forest Green
243	R	988	Forest Green-med.
246	▲	319	Pistachio Green-vy. dk.
307	Y	977	Golden Brown-lt.

Graphs begin on page 72.

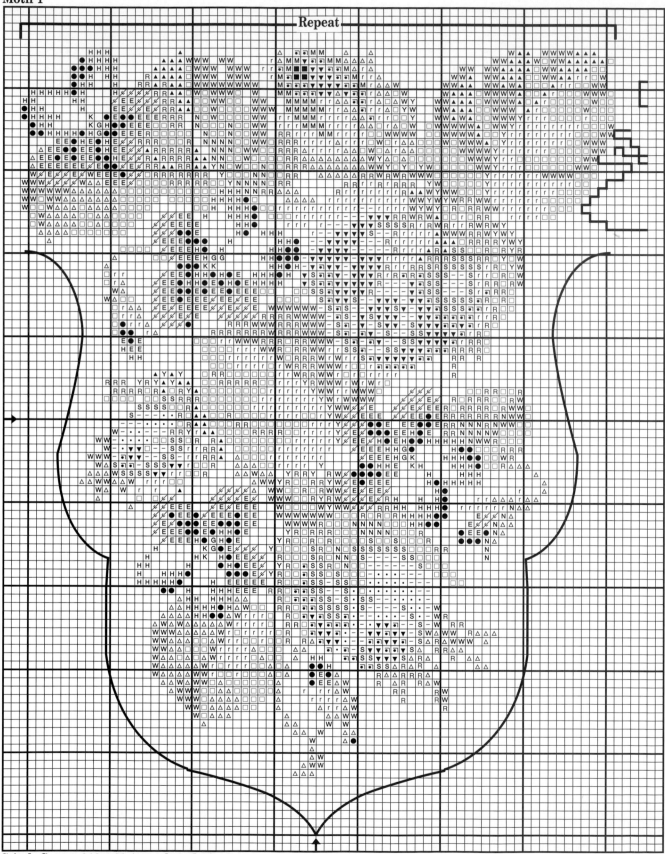

Stitch Count: 218 x 89 (complete design)

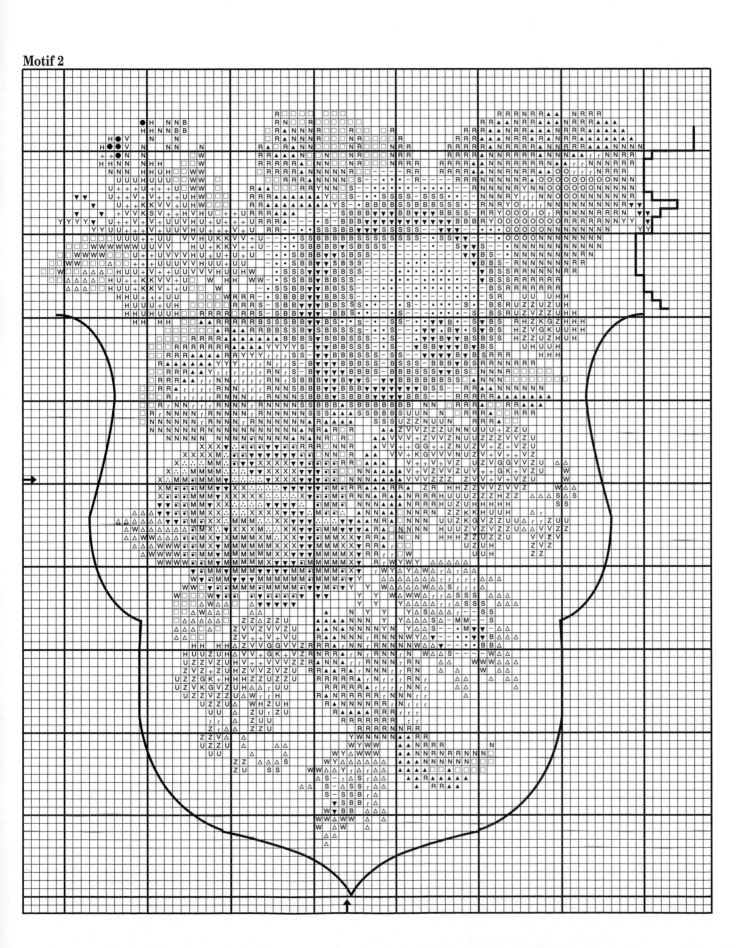

Father's Day

Surprise Dad with your artistry by making him this rustic sampler. The classic Northwestern design will complement his den, office, or favorite book nook. Another terrific idea: cover a photo album with the finished design piece.

Just for Dad

SAMPLE
Stitched on raw 32-count Belfast Linen over 2 threads, the finished design size is 6" x 8". The fabric was cut 12" x 14".

FABRICS	DESIGN SIZES
11-count	8⅞" x 11½"
14-count	6⅞" x 9⅛"
18-count	5⅜" x 7"
22-count	4⅜" x 5¾"

BONUS STITCHES
To make the photo album shown at right, center the design piece on the front cover of an album. Fold the left raw edge to the back of the design piece and press. Glue the design piece to the album cover along the folded edge of the fabric. Fold the remaining edges to the back of the front cover and glue.

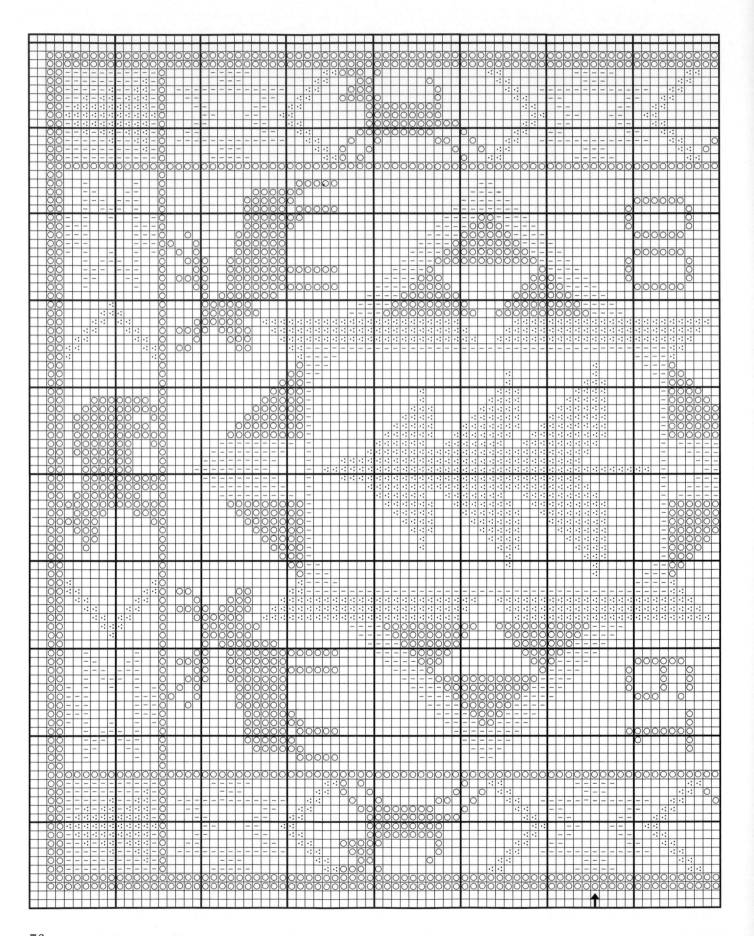

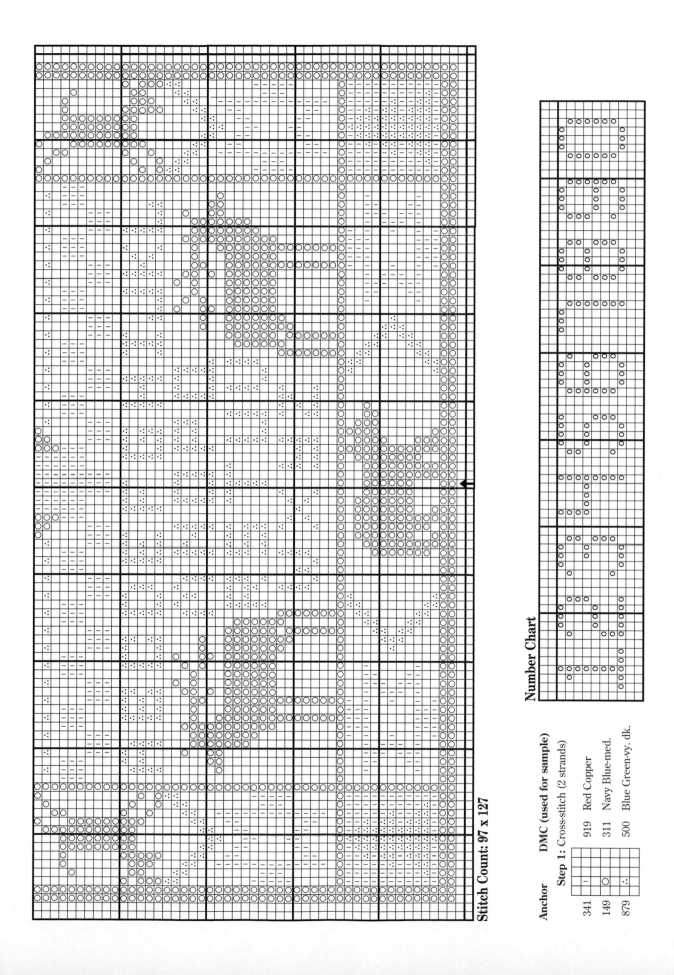

Stitch Count: 97 x 127

Number Chart

Anchor	DMC (used for sample)

Step 1: Cross-stitch (2 strands)

		Anchor	DMC	
−		341	919	Red Copper
O		149	311	Navy Blue-med.
∴		879	500	Blue Green-vy. dk.

Independence Day

Our grand old flag inspired these next two projects: The heartwarming pillow, *below*, will herald your patriotism throughout the year, and the cross-stitched and stenciled apron, *page 80*, is ideal for the chef of the neighborhood barbecue.

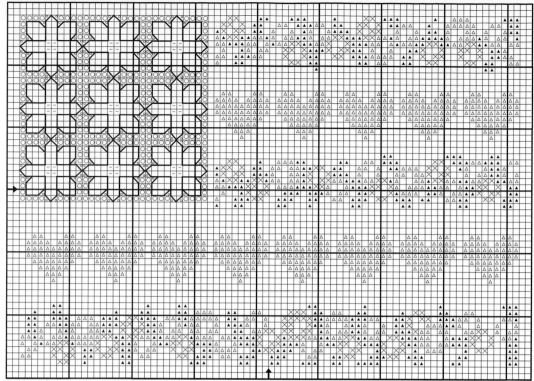

Stitch Count: 80 x 56

Patriotic Pillow

SAMPLE

Stitched on white 7-count Herta over 1 thread, the finished design size is 11½" x 8". The fabric was cut 18" x 14". See Suppliers, page 144, for DMC pearl cotton.

FABRICS	DESIGN SIZES
11-count	7¼" x 5⅛"
14-count	5¾" x 4"
18-count	4½" x 3⅛"
22-count	3⅝" x 2½"

MATERIALS

Completed cross-stitch on
   white 7-count Herta
2⅜ yards 45"-wide plaid fabric;
   matching thread
¼ yard floral fabric
50" length ¼" cording
2 (15¼" x 11¼") pieces fleece
Polyester stuffing

DIRECTIONS

All seam allowances are ¼".

1. With design centered, trim design piece to 15¼" x 11¼". Using design piece as pattern, cut pillow back from plaid fabric. From remainder, cut 8"-wide bias strips, piecing as needed to equal 3½ yards. From floral fabric, cut 1½"-wide bias strips, piecing as needed to equal 50".

2. Baste 1 fleece piece each to wrong side of design piece and pillow back.

3. Using pieced strip of floral fabric and cording, make 50" of corded piping (see page 136). With raw edges aligned, stitch piping to right side of design piece, clipping seam allowance of piping to round corners slightly.

4. For ruffle, with wrong sides facing, fold pieced plaid strip in half lengthwise and press. Run gathering thread along doubled raw edge of strip; pull to gather ruffle to fit around design piece. Secure

threads. With raw edges aligned, stitch ruffle to right side of design piece along stitching line of piping.

5. With right sides facing, raw edges aligned, and piping and ruffle toward center, stitch pillow back to design piece along stitching line of piping and ruffle, leaving an opening for turning. Trim fleece from seam allowance.

6. Turn and stuff firmly. Slipstitch opening closed.

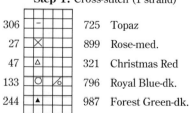

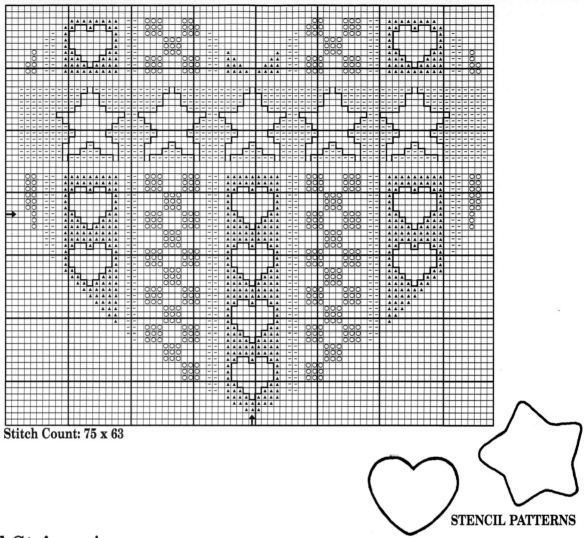

Stitch Count: 75 x 63

STENCIL PATTERNS

Stars-and-Stripes Apron

SAMPLE
Stitched on the bib piece of a purchased natural 14-count Adult Bib Apron over 1 thread, the finished design size is 5⅜" x 4½". See Suppliers, page 144, for the apron kit. Following the manufacturer's directions, attach the design piece to the apron.

FABRICS and DESIGN SIZES

FABRICS	DESIGN SIZES
11-count	6⅞" x 5¾"
14-count	5⅜" x 4½"
18-count	4⅛" x 3½"
22-count	3⅜" x 2⅞"

MATERIALS
Completed cross-stitch on natural 14-count Adult Bib Apron

1 yard ⅜"-wide deep burgundy grosgrain ribbon; matching thread
Tracing paper
Plastic template material
Cardboard scrap
Drafting tape
Craft knife
Acrylic fabric paints: rust, blue
Stencil brush

DIRECTIONS
1. From ribbon, cut 1 (8½") length, 1 (11½") length, and 1 (12½") length. Stitch 8½" length along top edge of stitched design, turning ends under ¼". Repeat to stitch 12½" length along bottom edge of design and 11½" length ¼" above bottom ribbon.

2. Transfer stencil patterns to template material and cut out. Using drafting tape, secure template material to cardboard. Using craft knife, cut out stencils.

3. Referring to photo, stencil stars and hearts as desired on apron pockets. Let dry.

Anchor		DMC	(used for sample)
Step 1: Cross-stitch (2 strands)			
47	O	321	Christmas Red
20	▲	498	Christmas Red-dk.
132	–	797	Royal Blue
Step 2: Backstitch (1 strand)			
20		498	Christmas Red-dk. (hearts)
132		797	Royal Blue (stars)

AUGUST 2
Friendship Day

Show a friend how much you care by working this delicate sampler. The soft pastel alphabet and lovely Hardanger stitches testify to a lasting friendship.

Love Letters

SAMPLE
Stitched on cream 32-count Belfast Linen over 2 threads, the finished design size is 9¼" x 10⅞". The fabric was cut 16" x 17". See Suppliers, page 144, for Waterlilies thread. See pages 138 and 139 for special stitches. See Framing Ideas, page 140.

FABRICS	DESIGN SIZES
11-count	13½" x 15⅞"
14-count	10⅝" x 12⅜"
18-count	8¼" x 9⅝"
22-count	6¾" x 7⅞"

Number Chart

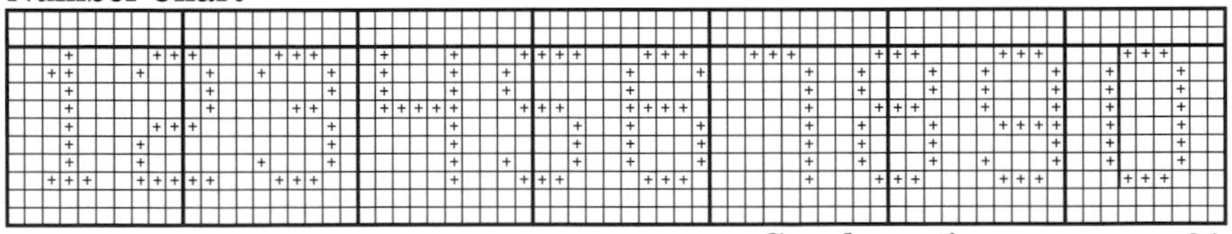

Graph continues on page 84.

TWISTED LADDER HEMSTITCH

SERPENTINE HEMSTITCH

SERPENTINE HEMSTITCH

Stitch Count: 148 x 174

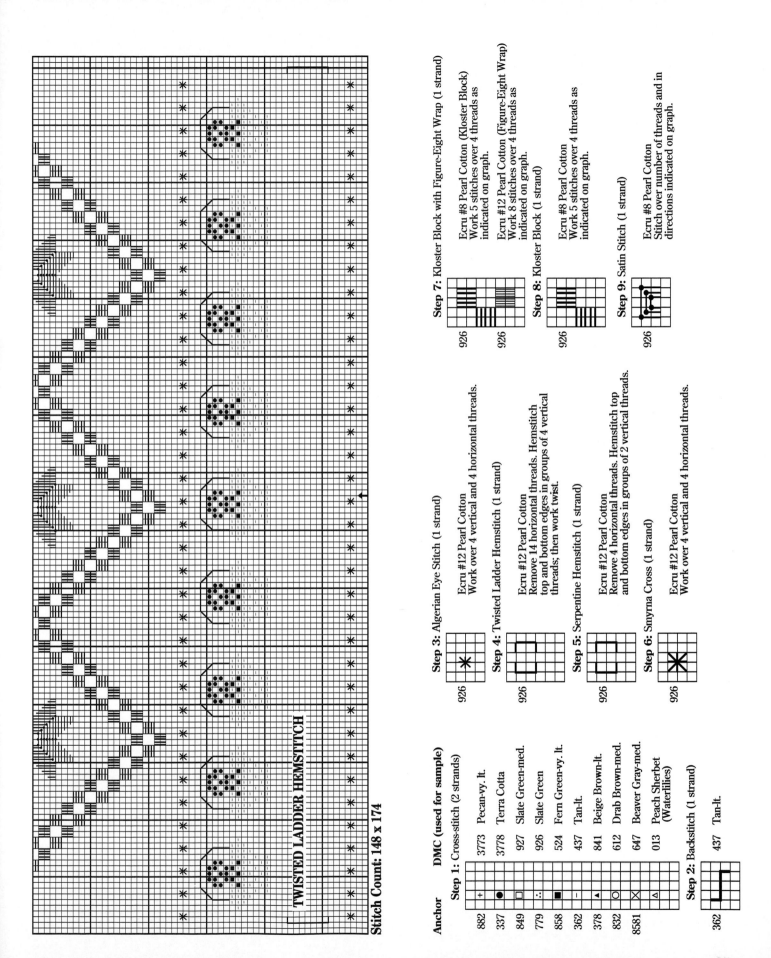

TWISTED LADDER HEMSTITCH

Anchor   **DMC (used for sample)**

Step 1: Cross-stitch (2 strands)

882	+	Pecan-vy. lt.
337	●	Terra Cotta
849	□	Slate Green-med.
779	∴	Slate Green
858	■	Fern Green-vy. lt.
362	–	Tan-lt.
378	▲	Beige Brown-lt.
832	○	Drab Brown-med.
8581	✕	Beaver Gray-med.
013	△	Peach Sherbet (Waterlilies)

Step 2: Backstitch (1 strand)

362		Tan-lt.

Step 3: Algerian Eye Stitch (1 strand)

926 — ✳

Ecru #12 Pearl Cotton
Work over 4 vertical and 4 horizontal threads.

Step 4: Twisted Ladder Hemstitch (1 strand)

926

Ecru #12 Pearl Cotton
Remove 14 horizontal threads. Hemstitch
top and bottom edges in groups of 4 vertical
threads; then work twist.

Step 5: Serpentine Hemstitch (1 strand)

926

Ecru #12 Pearl Cotton
Remove 4 horizontal threads. Hemstitch top
and bottom edges in groups of 2 vertical threads.

Step 6: Smyrna Cross (1 strand)

926 — ✖

Ecru #12 Pearl Cotton
Work over 4 vertical and 4 horizontal threads.

Step 7: Kloster Block with Figure-Eight Wrap (1 strand)

926

Ecru #8 Pearl Cotton (Kloster Block)
Work 5 stitches over 4 threads as
indicated on graph.

926

Ecru #12 Pearl Cotton (Figure-Eight Wrap)
Work 8 stitches over 4 threads as
indicated on graph.

Step 8: Kloster Block (1 strand)

926

Ecru #8 Pearl Cotton
Work 5 stitches over 4 threads as
indicated on graph.

Step 9: Satin Stitch (1 strand)

926

Ecru #8 Pearl Cotton
Stitch over number of threads and in
directions indicated on graph.

Grandparents' Day

Your grandparents will be honored when they set the table with a

pair of these sunny place mats designed by Trice Boerens.

Sunflower Place Mat

SAMPLE
Stitched on evergreen 28-count Linen over 2 threads, the finished design size is 12¼" x 8⅛". The fabric was cut 19" x 15".

FABRICS	DESIGN SIZES
11-count	15½" x 10⅜"
14-count	12¼" x 8⅛"
18-count	9½" x 6⅜"
22-count	7¾" x 5⅛"

MATERIALS (for 1 place mat)
Completed cross-stitch on evergreen 28-count Linen; matching thread
1 yard unstitched evergreen 28-count Linen
⅛ yard light green linen; matching thread
⅛ yard yellow fabric; matching thread
2⅛ yards ⅛" cording
⅜ yard fleece

DIRECTIONS
All seam allowances are ¼".
1. With design centered, trim design piece to 13½" x 8½". From unstitched 28-count Linen, cut 1 (13½" x 16") piece for top and 1 (13½" x 24") piece for backing. From light green linen, cut 1 (1" x 13½") strip. From remaining linen, cut 1½"-wide bias strips, piecing as needed to equal 78". From yellow fabric, cut ¾"-wide bias strips, piecing as needed to equal 75". From fleece, cut 1 (13½" x 24") piece.

2. Using pieced yellow strip and cording, make 75" of corded piping (see page 136).

3. To make place mat top, with wrong sides facing, fold 1" x 13½" light green strip in half lengthwise and press. With raw edges aligned, stitch strip to right side of design piece along top edge. With right sides facing and raw edges aligned, stitch 13½" x 16" piece of unstitched Linen to design piece along stitching line of light green strip. Press light green strip towards unstitched Linen.

4. With raw edges aligned, stitch piping to right side of place mat top, clipping seam allowance of piping to round corners slightly.

5. Stack backing (right side down), fleece, and top (right side up). Baste. For binding, with right sides facing, raw edges aligned, and piping toward center, stitch 78" pieced light green strip to top along stitching line of piping, mitering corners.

6. Fold raw edge of binding under ¼" and press. Fold binding ½" to back. Slipstitch pressed edge to backing, mitering corners.

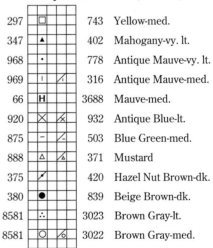

Anchor		DMC (used for sample)
Step 1: Cross-stitch (2 strands)		
297	□	743 Yellow-med.
347	▲	402 Mahogany-vy. lt.
968	·	778 Antique Mauve-vy. lt.
969	I ╱	316 Antique Mauve-med.
66	H	3688 Mauve-med.
920	╳ ╱	932 Antique Blue-lt.
875	− ╱	503 Blue Green-med.
888	△ ╱	371 Mustard
375	╱	420 Hazel Nut Brown-dk.
380	●	839 Beige Brown-dk.
8581	∴	3023 Brown Gray-lt.
8581	○ ╱	3022 Brown Gray-med.

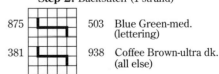

	Step 2: Backstitch (1 strand)	
875		503 Blue Green-med. (lettering)
381		938 Coffee Brown-ultra dk. (all else)

Graph begins on page 88.

Stitch Count: 171 x 114

Farm Animal Week

No barnyard is complete without hens and roosters clucking in the chicken coop. This cross-stitched pair could roost in your kitchen or breakfast room.

Fowl Play

SAMPLE for Design 1
Stitched on oatmeal 14-count
Floba over 1 thread, the fin-
ished design size for the hen
and rooster piece is 5¾" x 6⅜".
The fabric was cut 12" x 13".
See Framing Ideas, page 140.

FABRICS	DESIGN SIZES
11-count	7⅜" x 8⅛"
18-count	4½" x 5"
22-count	3⅝" x 4⅛"

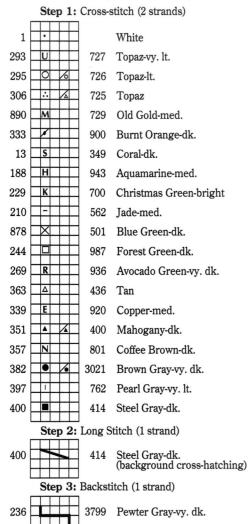

Anchor		DMC	(used for sample)

Step 1: Cross-stitch (2 strands)

1	·		White
293	U	727	Topaz-vy. lt.
295	O ◢	726	Topaz-lt.
306	∴ ◿	725	Topaz
890	M	729	Old Gold-med.
333	◿	900	Burnt Orange-dk.
13	S	349	Coral-dk.
188	H	943	Aquamarine-med.
229	K	700	Christmas Green-bright
210	–	562	Jade-med.
878	X	501	Blue Green-dk.
244	□	987	Forest Green-dk.
269	R	936	Avocado Green-vy. dk.
363	△	436	Tan
339	E	920	Copper-med.
351	▲ ◿	400	Mahogany-dk.
357	N	801	Coffee Brown-dk.
382	● ◢	3021	Brown Gray-vy. dk.
397	I	762	Pearl Gray-vy. lt.
400	■	414	Steel Gray-dk.

Step 2: Long Stitch (1 strand)

| 400 | ╱ | 414 | Steel Gray-dk. (background cross-hatching) |

Step 3: Backstitch (1 strand)

| 236 | | 3799 | Pewter Gray-vy. dk. |

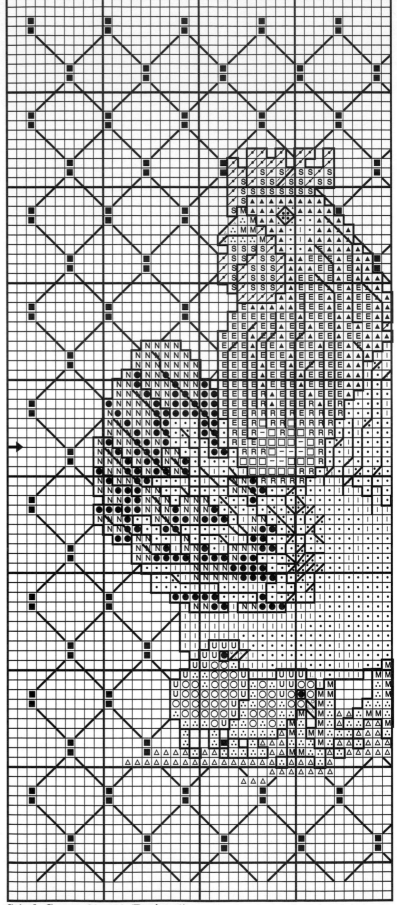

Stitch Count: 80 x 90 (Design 1)

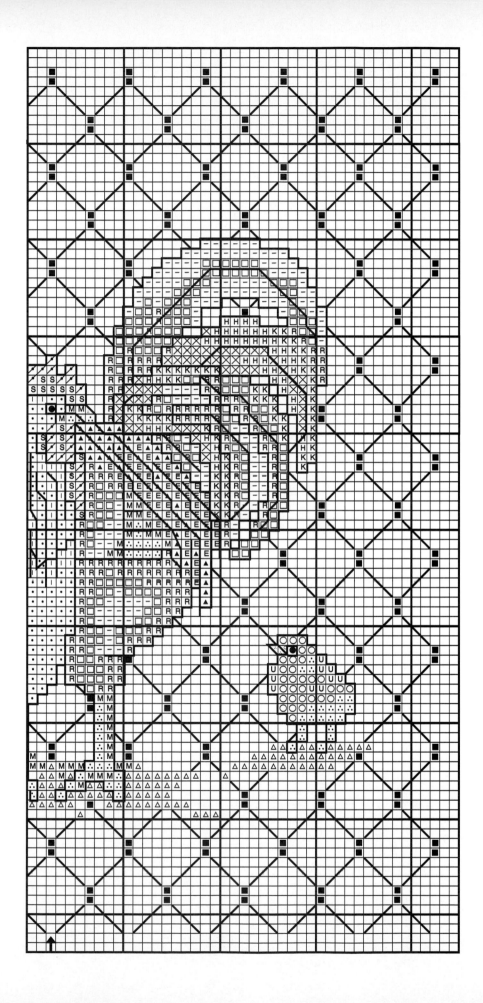

SAMPLE for Design 2

Stitched on oatmeal 14-count Floba over 1 thread, the finished design size for the nesting chickens piece is 5¾" x 6⅜". The fabric was cut 12" x 13". See Framing Ideas, page 140.

FABRICS	DESIGN SIZES
11-count	7¼" x 8⅛"
18-count	4½" x 5"
22-count	3⅝" x 4⅛"

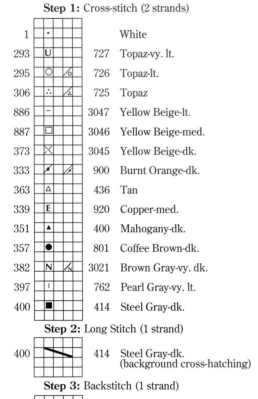

Anchor		DMC (used for sample)	

Step 1: Cross-stitch (2 strands)

1	·		White
293	U	727	Topaz-vy. lt.
295	O ⁄	726	Topaz-lt.
306	∴ ⁄	725	Topaz
886	–	3047	Yellow Beige-lt.
887	□	3046	Yellow Beige-med.
373	✕	3045	Yellow Beige-dk.
333	◢ ⁄	900	Burnt Orange-dk.
363	△	436	Tan
339	E	920	Copper-med.
351	▲	400	Mahogany-dk.
357	●	801	Coffee Brown-dk.
382	N ◺	3021	Brown Gray-vy. dk.
397	I	762	Pearl Gray-vy. lt.
400	■	414	Steel Gray-dk.

Step 2: Long Stitch (1 strand)

| 400 | | 414 | Steel Gray-dk. (background cross-hatching) |

Step 3: Backstitch (1 strand)

| 236 | | 3799 | Pewter Gray-vy. dk. |

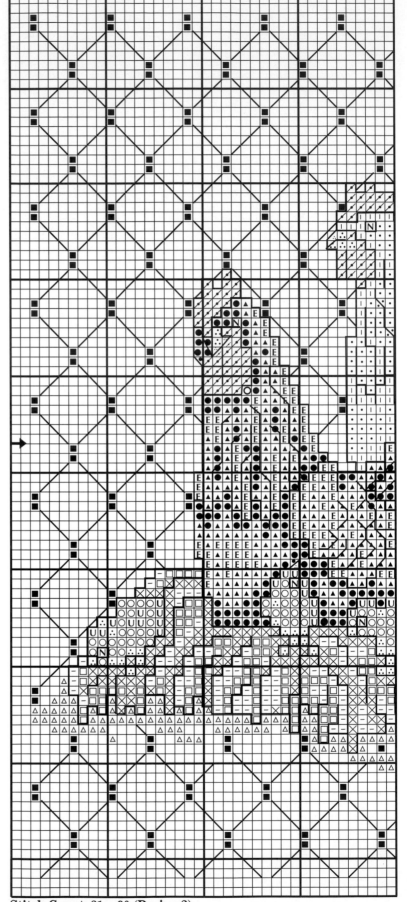

Stitch Count: 81 x 90 (Design 2)

National Dessert Day

Three little pigs stitched in sherbet colors are a sly reminder of how hard it is to resist the sweet temptation of dessert.

Dieter's Prayer

SAMPLE
Stitched on aqua 14-count Yorkshire over 1 thread, the finished design size is 7¼" x 3¼". The fabric was cut 14" x 10". See Framing Ideas, page 140.

FABRICS	DESIGN SIZES
11-count	9¼" x 4⅛"
18-count	5⅝" x 2½"
22-count	4⅝" x 2⅛"

Anchor			DMC	(used for sample)

Step 1: Cross-stitch (2 strands)

Anchor			DMC	
1				White
50			605	Cranberry-vy. lt.
76			603	Cranberry
78			601	Cranberry-dk.
118			340	Blue Violet-med.
928			598	Turquoise-lt.
400			414	Steel Gray-dk.

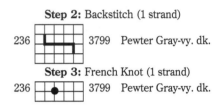

Step 2: Backstitch (1 strand)

		DMC	
236		3799	Pewter Gray-vy. dk.

Step 3: French Knot (1 strand)

		DMC	
236		3799	Pewter Gray-vy. dk.

Stitch Count: 102 x 46

OCTOBER 31
Halloween

Black cats and white ghosts follow a candy corn road around this trick-or-treat bucket. To repeat the theme, stencil Halloween motifs on the sides and the lid of the can.

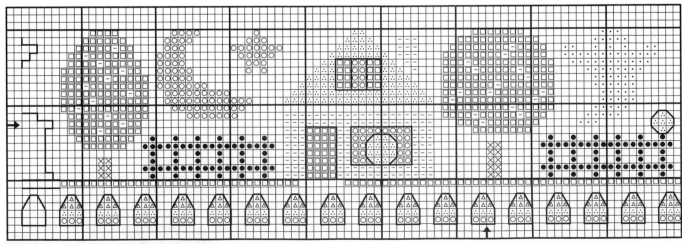

Stitch Count: 114 x 27 (for 1 repeat)

Boo Bucket Band

SAMPLE
Stitched on ebony 14-count Damask Aida over 1 thread, the finished design size for 1 repeat is 8⅛" x 1⅞". See steps 1 and 2 of Directions before cutting and stitching fabric.

FABRICS
FABRICS	DESIGN SIZES
11-count	10⅜" x 2½"
18-count	6⅜" x 1½"
22-count	5⅛" x 1¼"

MATERIALS
Completed cross-stitch design on ebony 14-count Damask Aida; matching thread
Unused 1-gallon paint can with handle and lid (often available from paint stores)
Spray primer
Acrylic paints: purple, black, yellow
Paintbrush
Stencil brush
Tracing paper
Plastic template material
Cardboard scrap
Drafting tape
Craft knife

DIRECTIONS
All seam allowances are ¼".

1. Before stitching design, measure circumference of can at center. Add 6" each to horizontal and vertical measurements. Cut 1 piece of unstitched Damask Aida to match measurements.

2. Center design vertically and begin stitching first motif 2¼" from 1 end of fabric. Repeat motif across fabric, leaving 2¼" unstitched at opposite end.

3. To make band, trim long edges of fabric 1½" above and below design. Trim 2" from each end. With right sides facing and raw edges aligned, fold design piece in half lengthwise. Stitch long edges together to make a tube. Turn. Center seam at back and press. Set aside.

4. Spray can with primer and let dry. Paint can with 2 coats of purple, letting paint dry between coats.

5. Transfer stencil patterns to template material. Using drafting tape, secure template material to cardboard. Using craft knife, cut out stencils.

6. Referring to photo, stencil yellow stars and moon as desired around top edge of can; stencil black cats around base of can and around lid. Let dry.

7. Fold raw ends of design piece under ¼" and press. Wrap band snugly around can, overlapping ends and aligning long edges. Slipstitch ends together.

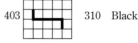

Anchor			DMC	(used for sample)
Step 1: Cross-stitch (2 strands)				
1				White
1				White (1 strand)
297			743	Yellow-med.
316			970	Pumpkin-lt.
349			921	Copper
98			553	Violet-med.
130			799	Delft-med.
227			701	Christmas Green-lt.
Step 2: Backstitch (1 strand)				
403			310	Black

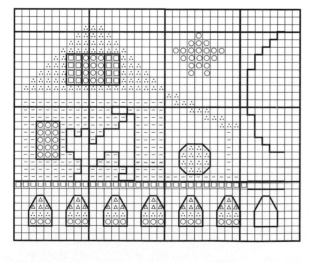

STENCIL PATTERNS

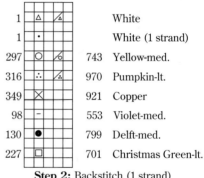

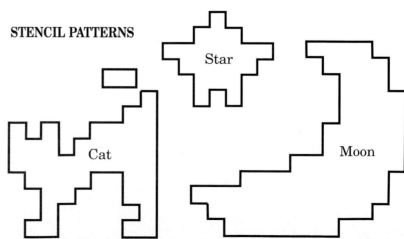

Star

Cat

Moon

International Gift Festival

Artisans from over thirty countries gather each year in Fairfield, Pennsylvania, to show their handcrafts. This sumptuous pair of seat cushion covers, inspired by Victorian needlepoint, are worthy of exhibition.

Floral Fantasies

SAMPLE for Design 1
Stitched on amber 32-count Linen over 2 threads, the finished design size is 10" x 10". The fabric was cut 20" x 20". Center and attach design piece to seat cushion as desired.

FABRICS	DESIGN SIZES
11-count	14½" x 14½"
14-count	11⅜" x 11⅜"
18-count	8⅞" x 8⅞"
22-count	7¼" x 7¼"

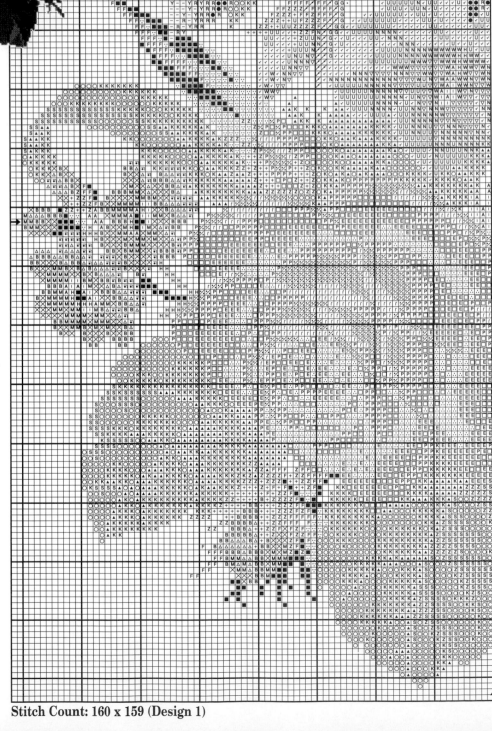

Stitch Count: 160 x 159 (Design 1)

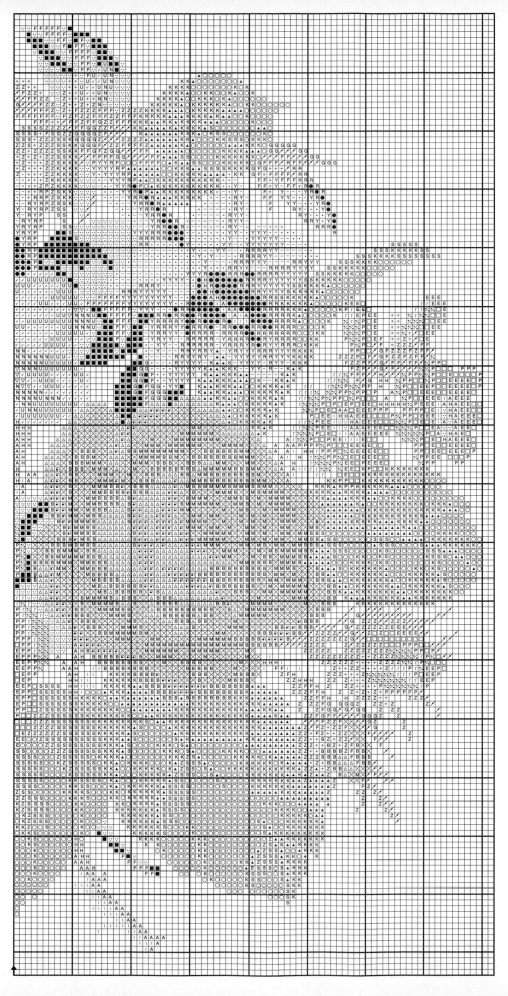

Anchor		DMC (used for sample)	

Step 1: Cross-stitch (2 strands)

Anchor		DMC	
387	✓	712	Cream
386	•	746	Off White
886	U	677	Old Gold-vy. lt.
891	N	676	Old Gold-lt.
890	▽	729	Old Gold-med.
901	W	680	Old Gold-dk.
881	I	945	Peach Beige
8	⊡	353	Peach
9	△	352	Coral-lt.
10	B	351	Coral
11	✕	3328	Salmon-dk.
13	M	347	Salmon-vy. dk.
892	⌐	819	Baby Pink-lt.
49	✕	963	Wild Rose-vy. lt.
50	P	3716	Wild Rose-lt.
76	☐	962	Wild Rose-med.
76	E	3731	Dusty Rose-med.
42	∴	3350	Dusty Rose-dk.
892	–	225	Shell Pink-vy. lt.
968	Y	778	Antique Mauve-vy. lt.
969	R	316	Antique Mauve-med.
970	●	3726	Antique Mauve-dk.
264	+	472	Avocado Green-ultra lt.
266	Z	471	Avocado Green-vy. lt.
844	F	3012	Khaki Green-med.
845	⁄	3011	Khaki Green-dk.
269	G	936	Avocado Green-vy. dk.
242	S	989	Forest Green
244	O	987	Forest Green-dk.
246	K	986	Forest Green-vy. dk.
879	▲	500	Blue Green-vy. dk.
347	A	402	Mahogany-vy. lt.
338	H	3776	Mahogany-lt.
370	∴	434	Brown-lt.
35	■	891	Carnation-dk.

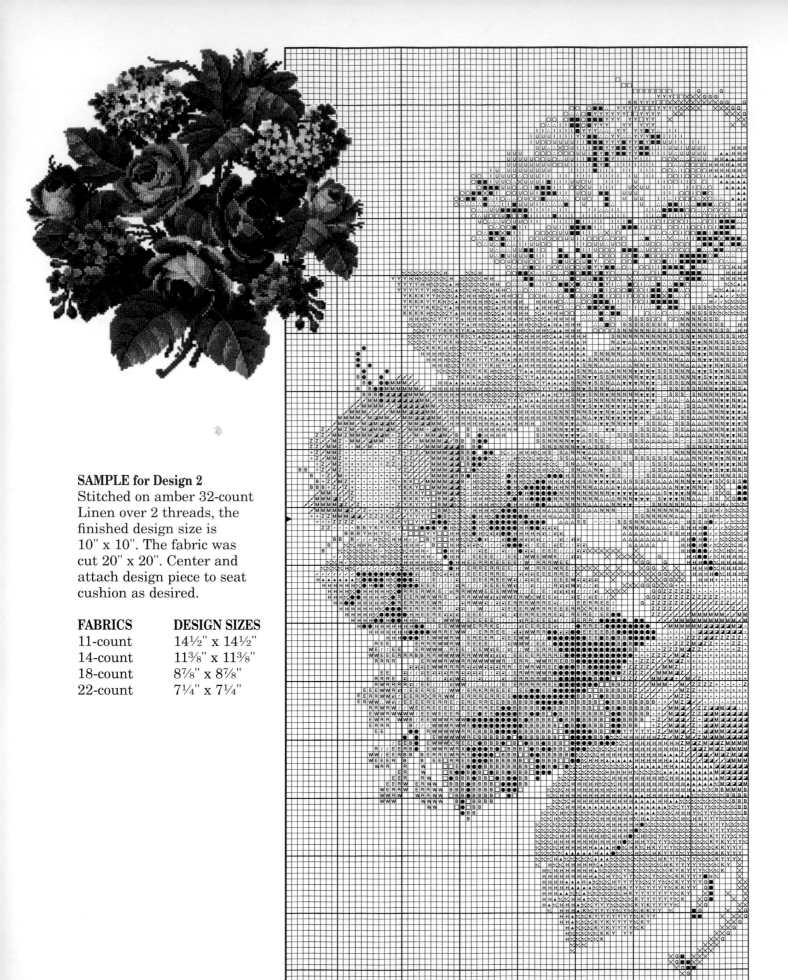

SAMPLE for Design 2
Stitched on amber 32-count
Linen over 2 threads, the
finished design size is
10" x 10". The fabric was
cut 20" x 20". Center and
attach design piece to seat
cushion as desired.

FABRICS	DESIGN SIZES
11-count	14½" x 14½"
14-count	11⅜" x 11⅜"
18-count	8⅞" x 8⅞"
22-count	7¼" x 7¼"

Stitch Count: 160 x 160 (Design 2)

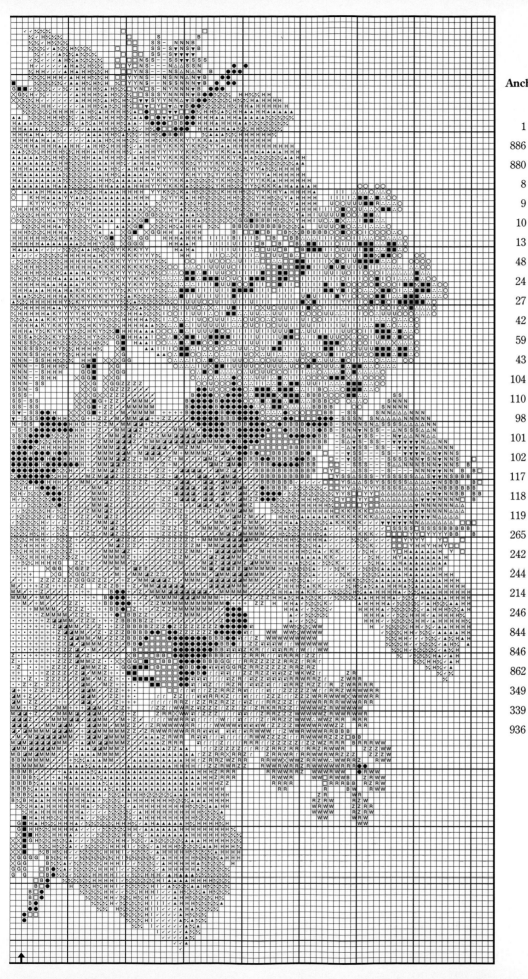

Thanksgiving

Give thanks this season
for the fellowship of
friends and family. The
cross-stitched homes in
our Thanksgiving town
call to mind the closeness
of community.

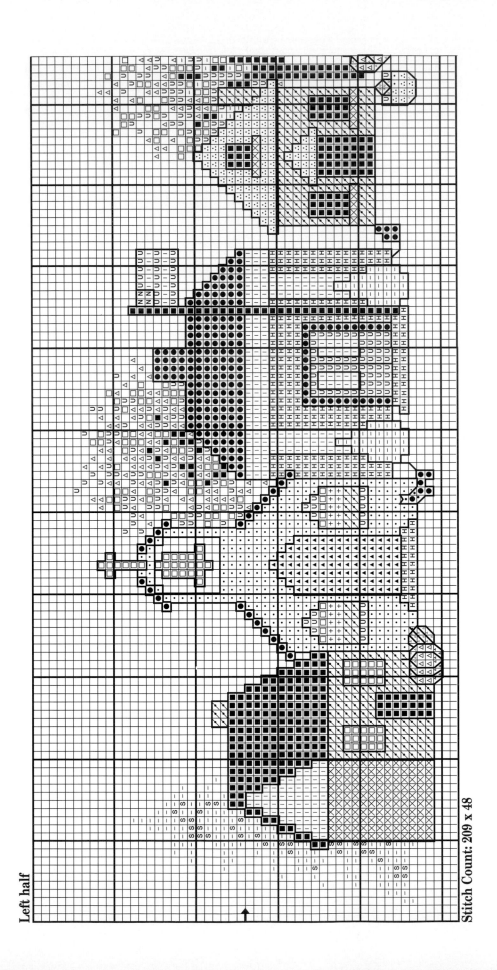

Left half

Stitch Count: 209 x 48

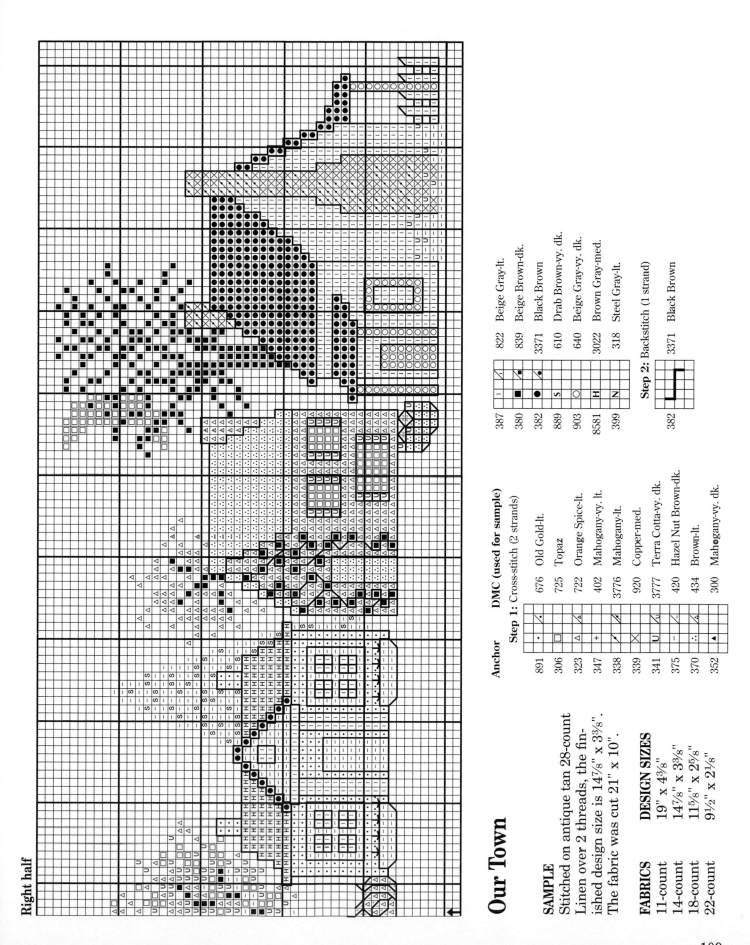

Our Town

SAMPLE

Stitched on antique tan 28-count
Linen over 2 threads, the fin-
ished design size is 14⅞" x 3⅜".
The fabric was cut 21" x 10".

FABRICS	DESIGN SIZES
11-count	19" x 4⅜"
14-count	14⅞" x 3⅜"
18-count	11⅝" x 2⅝"
22-count	9½" x 2⅛"

Anchor		DMC (used for sample)	
Step 1: Cross-stitch (2 strands)			
891	·	676	Old Gold-lt.
306	□	725	Topaz
323	⊿	722	Orange Spice-lt.
347	+	402	Mahogany-vy. lt.
338	◿	3776	Mahogany-lt.
339	⊠	920	Copper-med.
341	⊍	3777	Terra Cotta-vy. dk.
375	−	420	Hazel Nut Brown-dk.
370	∷	434	Brown-lt.
352	▲	300	Mahogany-vy. dk.
387	−	822	Beige Gray-lt.
380	■	839	Beige Brown-dk.
382	●	3371	Black Brown
889	S	610	Drab Brown-vy. dk.
903	○	640	Beige Gray-vy. lt.
8581	H	3022	Brown Gray-med.
399	N	318	Steel Gray-lt.
Step 2: Backstitch (1 strand)			
382		3371	Black Brown

Snowflake Festival

Klamath Falls, Oregon, celebrates the arrival of winter with nine chilly days of festivities. You can bring the freshness of new-fallen snow to your corner of the world with this sparkling pillow trimmed in frosty blue.

Snowflake Pillow

SAMPLE
Stitched on white 32-count Belfast Linen over 2 threads, the finished design size is 6" x 6¼". The fabric was cut 18" x 16". Begin stitching in upper left corner, with top and left edges of design each 5" from edge of fabric. See Suppliers, page 144, for Balger blending filament.

FABRICS	DESIGN SIZES
11-count	8¾" x 9⅛"
14-count	6⅞" x 7⅛"
18-count	5⅜" x 5½"
22-count	4⅜" x 4½"

MATERIALS
Completed cross-stitch on white 32-count Belfast Linen
½ yard light blue polished cotton; matching thread
2⅝ yards ¼"-wide light blue braided trim; matching thread
52" length ¼" cording
2 (14½" x 12½") pieces fleece
Polyester stuffing

DIRECTIONS
All seam allowances are ¼".

1. With top and left edges of stitched area each 1½" from edge of fabric, trim design piece to 14½" x 12½". Using design piece as pattern, cut pillow back from light blue cotton. From remainder, cut 1½"-wide bias strips, piecing as needed to equal 52".

2. Cut 1 length each from braided trim in the following order: 15½", 13½", 11½", 9", 7½", 14½", 12½", and 10". Referring to photo, pin first 5 lengths diagonally across lower right corner of design piece, spacing lengths approximately 1¼" apart. Referring to photo, pin remaining 3 lengths across first group, spacing lengths approximately 1¼" apart and weaving lengths in lattice fashion. Hand-stitch in place.

3. Using pieced strip of light blue cotton and cording, make 52" length of corded piping (see page 136). With raw edges aligned, stitch piping to right side of design piece, rounding corners.

4. Baste 1 fleece piece each to wrong side of design piece and pillow back.

5. With right sides facing, raw edges aligned, and piping toward center, stitch design piece to pillow back along stitching line of piping, leaving an opening for turning. Trim fleece from seam allowance. Turn and stuff moderately. Slipstitch opening closed.

Anchor	DMC (used for sample)

Step 1: Cross-stitch (4 strands)

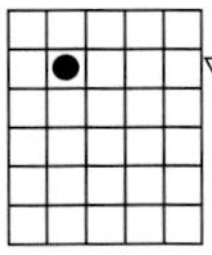

121   794   Cornflower Blue-lt. (2 strands)

032   Pearl Balger blending filament (2 strands)

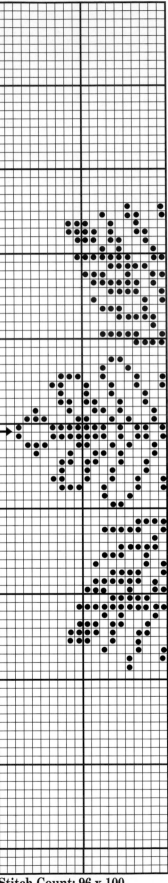

Stitch Count: 96 x 100

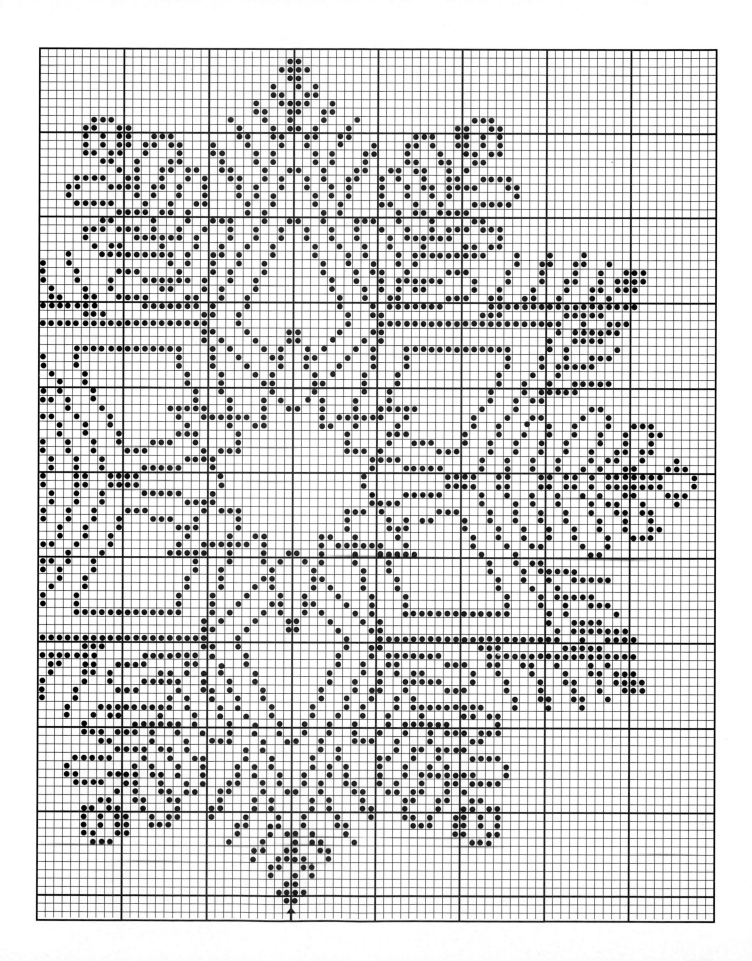

Winter Solstice

When winter blows its blustery winds, stay warm inside stitching a classic sampler. In this forest scene, cardinals serenade a starry night sky.

Winter Woodland

SAMPLE
Stitched on oatmeal 14-count Rustico over 1 thread, the finished design size is 10½" x 9⅛". The fabric was cut 17" x 16". Referring to photo, center and stitch desired name and date in heart. See Framing Ideas, page 140.

FABRICS
11-count
18-count
22-count

DESIGN SIZES
13⅜" x 11⅝"
8⅛" x 7⅛"
6⅝" x 5⅞"

Anchor			DMC (used for sample)	
Step 1: Cross-stitch (2 strands)				
387	+	⁄	712	Cream
300	·		745	Yellow-lt. pale
47	∴	⁄	321	Christmas Red
145	□		334	Baby Blue-med.
149	O	⁄	311	Navy Blue-med.
215	△	⁄	320	Pistachio Green-med.
212	●	⁄	561	Jade-vy. dk.
362	⁄	⁄	437	Tan-lt.
309	M	⁄M	435	Brown-vy. lt.
914	–	⁄	3772	Pecan-med.
379	✕	⁄	840	Beige Brown-med.
380	▲	⁄	839	Beige Brown-dk.
382	■	⁄	3371	Black Brown
900	I		648	Beaver Gray-lt.
Step 2: Backstitch (1 strand)				
382			3371	Black Brown
Step 3: French Knot (1 strand)				
382	●		3371	Black Brown

Graph begins on page 116.

Stitch Count: 147 x 128

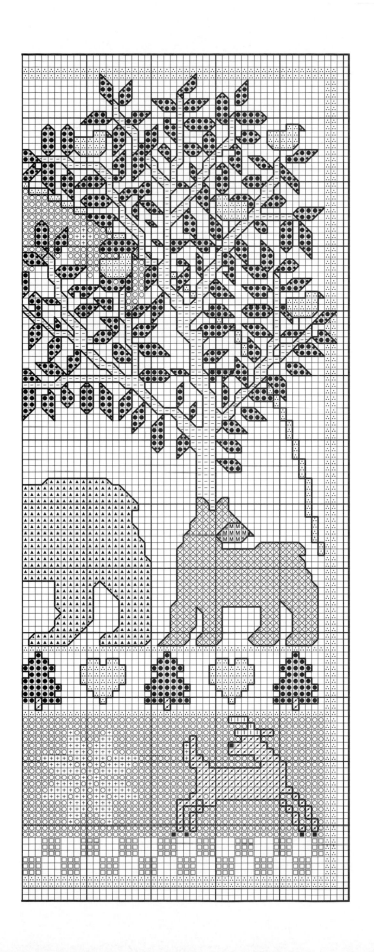

DECEMBER 24

Christmas Eve

Children love to stay up late in hopes of catching a glimpse of Santa, but they seem to always fall asleep before the jolly old man arrives. Designer Terrece Beesley has captured his visit in this endearing cross-stitched piece.

To All a Good Night

SAMPLE
Stitched on white 32-count Belfast Linen over 2 threads, the finished design size is 8¼" x 10¾". The fabric was cut 15" x 17".

FABRICS	DESIGN SIZES
11-count	11⅞" x 15¾"
14-count	9⅜" x 12⅜"
18-count	7¼" x 9⅝"
22-count	6" x 7⅞"

Anchor **DMC (used for sample)**

Step 1: Cross-stitch (2 strands)

Anchor	Symbol	DMC	Color
1	•		White
300	V	745	Yellow-lt. pale
891	⅜	676	Old Gold-lt.
887	B	3046	Yellow Beige-med.
373	M	3045	Yellow Beige-dk.
366	–	951	Peach Pecan-lt.
4146	/	754	Peach-lt.
868	U	758	Terra Cotta-lt.
9	Z	760	Salmon
13	▼	349	Coral-dk.
22	H	816	Garnet
44	∴	814	Garnet-dk.
101	I	327	Antique Violet-vy. dk.
920	W	932	Antique Blue-lt.
920	S	932	Antique Blue-lt. (1 strand)
130	Y	799	Delft-med.
940	K	792	Cornflower Blue-dk.
149	▲	336	Navy Blue
849	□	927	Slate Green-med.
266	○	471	Avocado Green-vy. lt.
242	E	989	Forest Green
210	△	562	Jade-med.
878	N	501	Blue Green-dk.
879	●	500	Blue Green-vy. dk.
338	◘	3776	Mahogany-lt.
351	R	400	Mahogany-dk.
352	╳	300	Mahogany-vy. dk.
381	■	838	Beige Brown-vy. dk.
397	+	762	Pearl Gray-vy. lt.
398	G	415	Pearl Gray

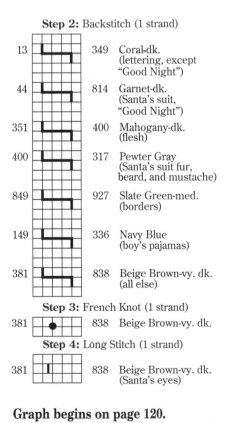

Step 2: Backstitch (1 strand)

Anchor	DMC	Color
13	349	Coral-dk. (lettering, except "Good Night")
44	814	Garnet-dk. (Santa's suit, "Good Night")
351	400	Mahogany-dk. (flesh)
400	317	Pewter Gray (Santa's suit fur, beard, and mustache)
849	927	Slate Green-med. (borders)
149	336	Navy Blue (boy's pajamas)
381	838	Beige Brown-vy. dk. (all else)

Step 3: French Knot (1 strand)

Anchor	DMC	Color
381	838	Beige Brown-vy. dk.

Step 4: Long Stitch (1 strand)

Anchor	DMC	Color
381	838	Beige Brown-vy. dk. (Santa's eyes)

Graph begins on page 120.

121

Lower half

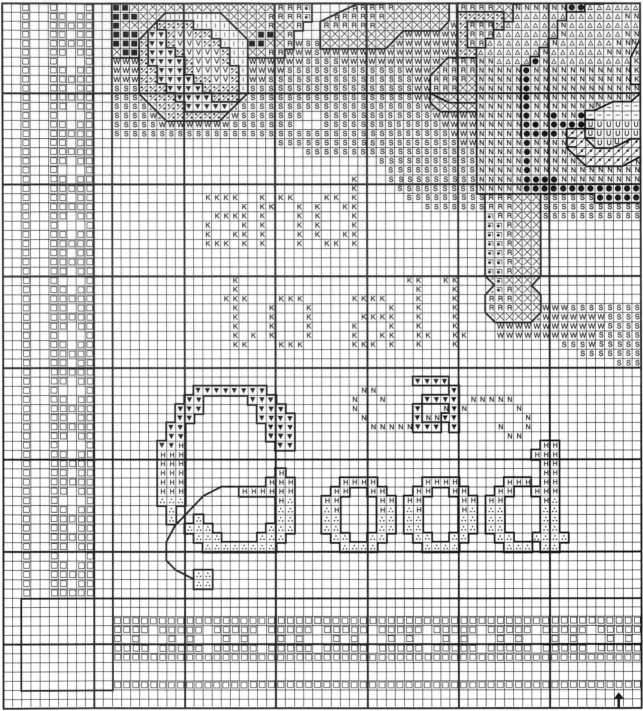

Stitch Count: 131 x 173

DECEMBER 25

Christmas Day

Bring to Christmas the charm of handmade gifts and decorations with an oversize stocking in rich, woodsy colors, *shown at left*, a crocheted and cross-stitched muffler, *page 128*, and a winsome Santa sampler, *page 130*.

For You, My Deer

SAMPLE

Stitched on ruby red and evergreen 28-count Linen over 2 threads, the finished design size for the complete design is 6⅜" x 6½". See steps 2 and 3 of the Directions before cutting and stitching fabric.

FABRICS	DESIGN SIZES
11-count	8⅛" x 8¼"
14-count	6⅜" x 6½"
18-count	5" x 5"
22-count	4⅛" x 4⅛"

MATERIALS

⅜ yard ruby red 28-count Linen; matching thread
⅜ yard evergreen 28-count Linen; matching thread
¼ yard 45"-wide tan linen; matching thread
⅜ yard 45"-wide dark red fabric
8 assorted ¾" brown and green buttons
Tracing paper
Dressmaker's pen

DIRECTIONS

All seam allowances are ½". Pattern includes ¼" seam allowance.

1. Enlarge stocking pattern and transfer to tracing paper; cut out.

2. Cut 2 (11" x 13") pieces from ruby red Linen and 2 (9¾" x 13") pieces from evergreen Linen. From tan linen, cut 1 (8½" x 20") piece for cuff and 1 (1" x 5") strip for hanger. From dark red fabric, cut 2 stocking pieces for lining.

3. For stocking front, join 1 ruby red Linen piece to 1 evergreen Linen piece, stitching together along 1 (13") edge. Press seam open. Repeat with remaining ruby red and evergreen Linen pieces for stocking back.

4. Referring to photo, with deer design centered horizontally on stocking front, begin stitching bottom edge of design ½" below seam on evergreen Linen. Continue stitching

design over seam and onto ruby red Linen.

5. With wrong sides facing and raw edges and middle seams aligned, baste stocking front to back. Pin pattern to stocking front, with design centered horizontally and middle seam placement line on pattern aligned with seam on stocking front. Cut through both layers for stocking front and back. Remove basting. Referring to photo, sew buttons to stocking front below design.

6. With right sides facing and raw edges aligned, stitch stocking front to back, leaving top edge open. Turn.

7. For cuff, with raw edges aligned, stitch short edges of cuff piece together. Press seam open. With wrong sides facing and long raw edges aligned, fold cuff in half; press. With folded edge at bottom, slide cuff over stocking, aligning raw edges, and matching cuff seam to side seam of stocking above heel. Baste cuff to stocking around top edge.

8. For hanger, with raw edges aligned, fold hanger piece in half lengthwise. Stitch long edges together; turn. Center seam and press. Fold in half to make a loop. With raw edges aligned and loop toward center, baste hanger to right side of cuff on stocking back at top corner above heel.

9. For lining, with right sides facing and raw edges aligned, stitch lining pieces together, leaving top edge open and a large opening in seam above heel. Clip curves but do not turn. With right sides facing, slide lining over stocking and cuff, matching seams. With raw edges aligned, stitch along top edge of stocking, securing cuff and hanger in seam. Turn

through opening in lining. Slipstitch opening closed. Tuck lining inside stocking. Turn down cuff and press.

Anchor			DMC (used for sample)	
Step 1: Cross-stitch (2 strands)				
885	·	⁄	739	Tan-ultra vy. lt.
942	△	⁄	738	Tan-vy. lt.
942	−		738	Tan-vy. lt. (1 strand)
376			842	Beige Brown-vy. lt. (1 strand)
378	○	⁄	841	Beige Brown-lt.
379	✕	⁄	840	Beige Brown-med.
273	∴	⁄	3787	Brown Gray-dk.
382	●	⁄	3371	Black Brown
Step 2: Backstitch (1 strand)				
376			842	Beige Brown-vy. lt. (eyes)

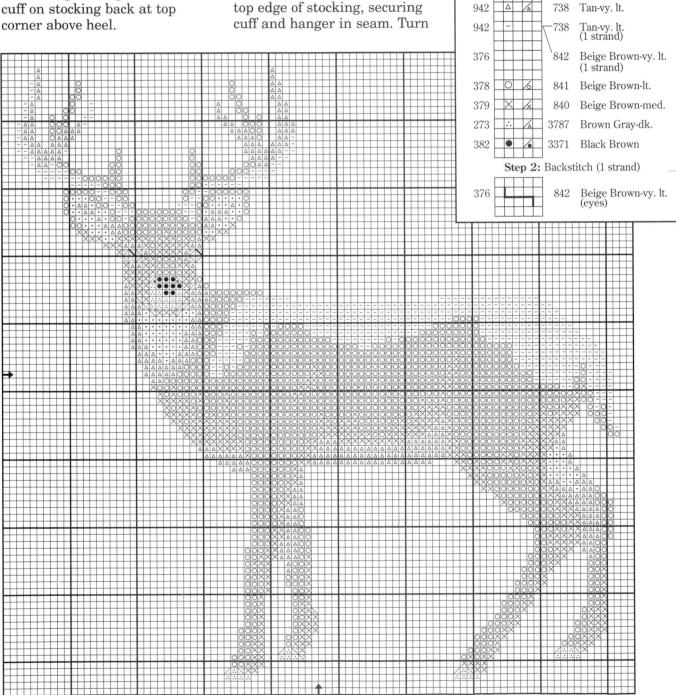

Stitch Count: 90 x 91

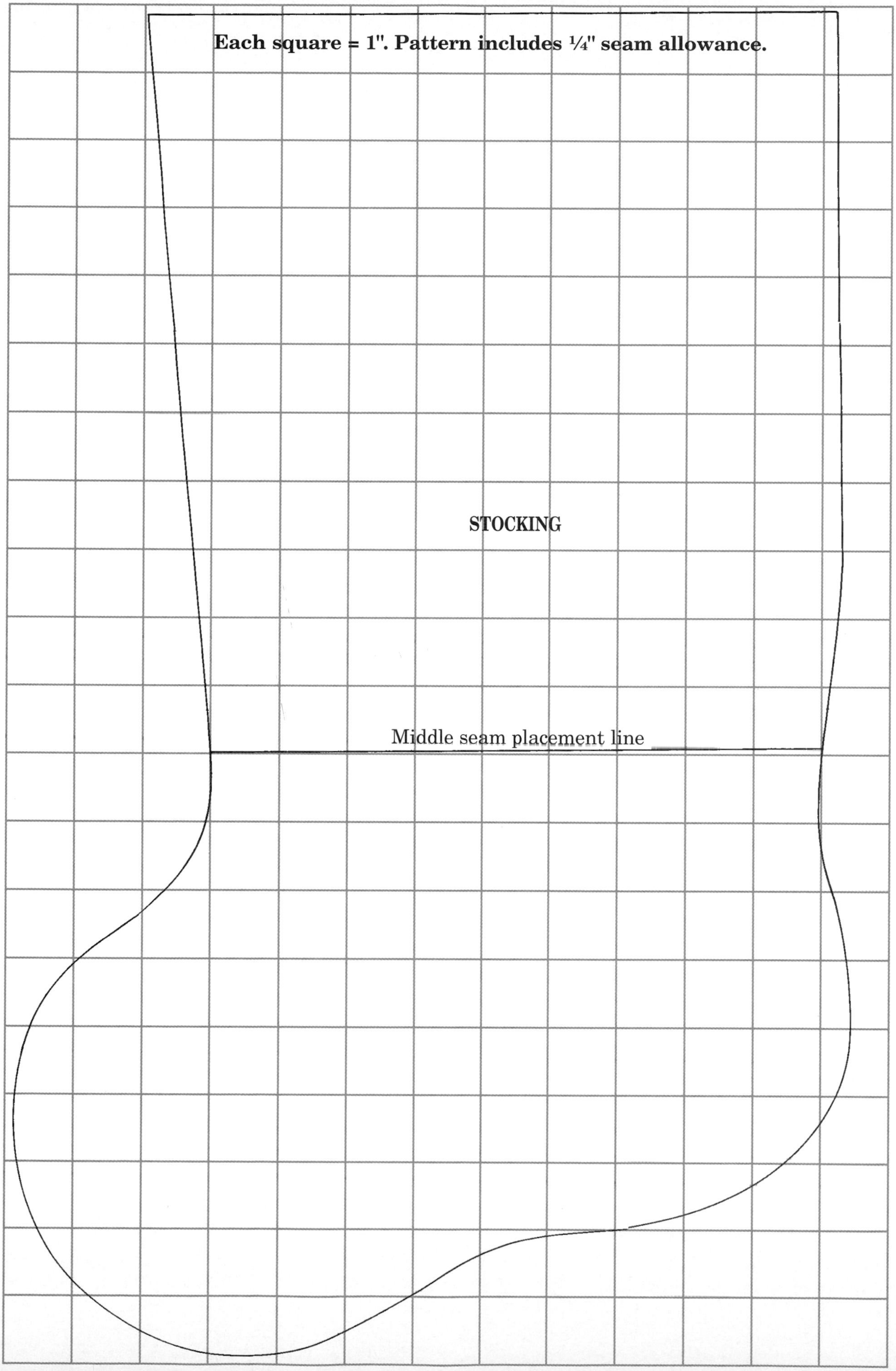

Each square = 1". Pattern includes ¼" seam allowance.

STOCKING

Middle seam placement line

Cozy Cardinal Muffler

SAMPLE (for cross-stitch)
Stitched on crocheted muffler, the finished design size is 5¾" x 9⅝". With design centered horizontally, begin stitching bottom edge of design 1 row of crochet stitches above each end of muffler. See Suppliers, page 144, for Paternayan Persian yarn used in cross-stitch.

Crochet Instructions

MATERIALS
6 (50-gram, 115-yard) skeins of worsted-weight wool-silk blend nubby yarn
Size F afghan hook (or size to obtain gauge)
Size E crochet hook

DIRECTIONS
Gauge: 9 sts and 9 rows = 2".
Finished size (for muffler): Approximately 6½" x 81" plus fringe.

MUFFLER: With size F afghan hook, ch 30. **Row 1: Step 1:** Keeping all lps on hook, pull up a lp through top lp only, in 2nd ch from hook and in ea ch across = 30 lps on hook. Do not turn. **Row 1: Step 2:** Yo and pull through first lp on hook, * yo and pull through 2 lps on hook, rep from * across (1 lp remains on hook for first lp of next row). Do not turn. **Row 2: Step 1:** Keeping all lps on hook, pull up a lp from under 2nd vertical bar,

* pull up a lp from under next vertical bar, rep from * across. Do not turn. **Row 2: Step 2:** Rep Step 2 of Row 1. Rep Steps 1 and 2 of Row 2 for 360 rows of afghan st (or desired length). **Last row:** Sl st in ea st across. Do not fasten off. **Border:** With size E crochet hook, ch 1, * sc in ea st across to corner of muffler, (sc, ch 1, sc) in corner, rep from * around, end with sl st in beg ch-1. Fasten off.

FRINGE: In every other stitch on each end of muffler, fold 3 (12") strands of yarn in half to make a loop. Pull loop through stitch to wrong side. Pull loose ends through loop and pull tightly to secure.

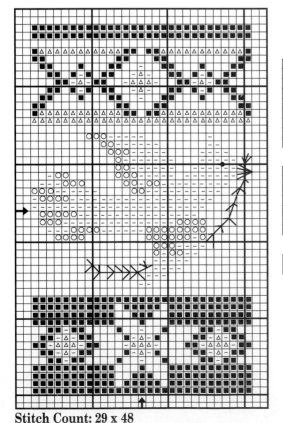

Stitch Count: 29 x 48

Paternayan Persian Yarn (used for sample)

Step 1: Cross-stitch (1 strand)

−	969	Christmas Red-dk.
O	940	Cranberry-vy. dk.
△	513	Old Blue
■	662	Pine Green

Step 2: Long Stitch (1 strand)

╱	733	Honey Gold (beak)
╱	662	Pine Green (leaves)

Step 3: French Knot (1 strand)

●	220	Black

CROCHET ABBREVIATIONS

ch—chain
ea—each
lp(s)—loop(s)
rep—repeat
sc—single crochet
sl st—slip stitch
st(s)—stitch(es)
yo—yarn over

But give me holly,
Bold and jolly,
Honest, prickly,
Shining holly;
Pluck me berry,
Leaf and berry,
For the day when
I make merry.
—Christina Rossetti

We Love Santa

SAMPLE
Stitched on white 14-count
Aida over 1 thread, the
finished design size is 10" x 8".
The fabric was cut 16" x 14".
See Framing Ideas, page 140.

FABRICS	DESIGN SIZES
11-count	12¾" x 10⅛"
18-count	7¾" x 6¼"
22-count	6⅜" x 5⅛"

BONUS STITCHES

Make delightful orna-
ments from the individual
motifs in this sampler:
Stitch a motif and cut it
out ¼" from the stitched
design. From red or green
fabric, cut out a matching
backing piece. With right
sides facing and raw edges
aligned, stitch the pieces
together with a ¼" seam,
leaving an opening for
turning. Turn and stuff
firmly. Tack a hanging loop
to the top of the ornament.

Stitch Count: 140 x 112

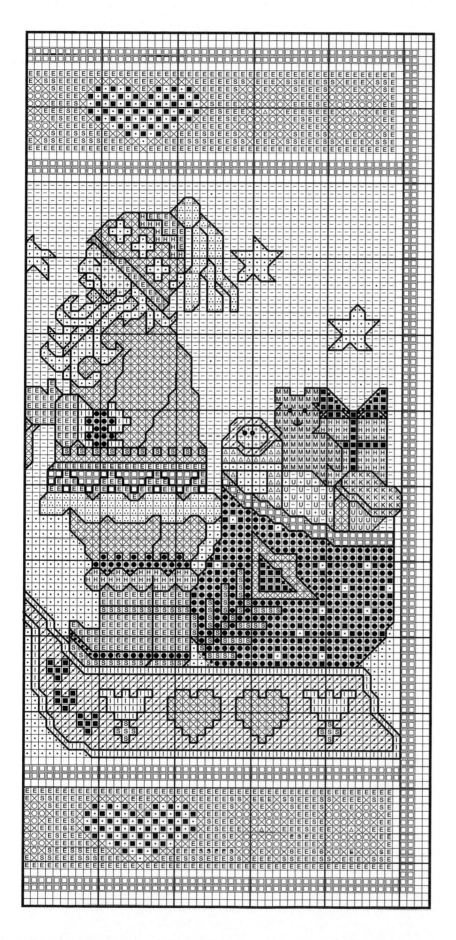

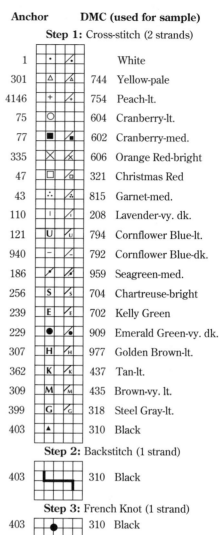

Anchor			DMC (used for sample)

Step 1: Cross-stitch (2 strands)

Anchor				DMC	
1	·	⁄			White
301	△	⁄△		744	Yellow-pale
4146	+	⁄+		754	Peach-lt.
75	○			604	Cranberry-lt.
77	■	⁄■		602	Cranberry-med.
335	✕	⁄✕		606	Orange Red-bright
47	☐	⁄□		321	Christmas Red
43	∴	⁄∴		815	Garnet-med.
110	I	⁄I		208	Lavender-vy. dk.
121	U	⁄U		794	Cornflower Blue-lt.
940	–	⁄		792	Cornflower Blue-dk.
186	⁄	⁄		959	Seagreen-med.
256	S	⁄S		704	Chartreuse-bright
239	E	⁄E		702	Kelly Green
229	●	⁄●		909	Emerald Green-vy. dk.
307	H	⁄H		977	Golden Brown-lt.
362	K	⁄K		437	Tan-lt.
309	M	⁄M		435	Brown-vy. lt.
399	G	⁄G		318	Steel Gray-lt.
403	▲			310	Black

Step 2: Backstitch (1 strand)

403	⌐	310	Black

Step 3: French Knot (1 strand)

403	●	310	Black

General Instructions

Use this step-by-step guide to help you achieve success with your cross-stitch projects.

CROSS-STITCH

Fabrics: Most designs in this book are worked on even-weave fabrics that are made especially for cross-stitch and can be found in your local needlework shop. If you cannot find a fabric, see Suppliers, page 144, for ordering information.

Fabrics used in models are identified in Sample information by color, thread count per inch, and name.

Finished Design Size: Finished design sizes are given for fabric used in sample and for 11-, 14-, 18-, and 22-count fabrics. To determine size of finished design on fabric other than those listed, divide stitch count by number of threads per inch of fabric. When design is stitched over 2 threads, divide stitch count by half the number of threads per inch.

Preparing Fabric: Cut fabric at least 3" larger on all sides than finished design size (or as indicated in Sample information) to ensure enough space for matting, framing, and other finishing techniques. To prevent fraying, whipstitch, machine-zigzag, or apply liquid ravel preventer to raw fabric edges.

Needles: Choose a blunt-tipped tapestry needle that will slip easily through fabric holes without piercing fabric threads.

For fabric with 11 or fewer threads per inch, use needle size 24; for 14 threads per inch, use size 24 or 26; and for 18 or more threads per inch, use size 26. Never leave needle in design area of work—it may leave rust or permanent impression on fabric.

Hoop or Frame: Use an embroidery hoop or stretcher bar frame to keep fabric taut and to help make uniform stitches.

page 24

Select hoop or frame large enough to hold entire design, if possible. Place screw or clamp of hoop in 10 o'clock position (or 2 o'clock if you are left-handed) to keep it from catching floss.

Graphs and Color Codes: On graphs, a square containing a symbol represents 1 stitch to be worked.

Each symbol corresponds to a specific color of embroidery floss, identified by name and number on color code. Flosses are cross-referenced, giving both DMC and Anchor color numbers.

Color codes also indicate stitches to be used and number of floss strands for each stitch. Stitch count for entire design is listed below each graph. Heavy lines on graphs indicate repeats.

Centering Design: To find center of fabric, fold it in half horizontally and then vertically. Place pin in intersection of folds to mark center. To find center of graph, follow vertical and horizontal arrows until they intersect. Begin stitching center of design in center of fabric (unless otherwise indicated).

134

Embroidery Floss: Use 18" lengths of floss (longer pieces tend to twist and knot). For best coverage, separate all 6 floss strands and dampen strands with wet sponge to straighten. Then recombine number of strands called for in color code. Floss covers best when lying flat. If floss begins to twist, suspend needle and allow floss to unwind.

Securing Floss: Bring needle and floss up through fabric, leaving 1" tail on underside. Secure floss tail with first few stitches.

Another method for securing floss is with a waste knot. Knot floss and bring needle down through fabric approximately 1" from where first stitch will be taken. Secure floss on back of fabric with first 4 or 5 stitches. After floss is secured, cut off knot from underside of fabric.

To secure floss after stitching is complete, run needle under 4 or 5 stitches on back of design and clip ends close to fabric.

Stitching Method: For smooth stitches, use push-and-pull method. Starting on wrong side of fabric, bring needle straight up, pulling floss completely through to right side. Reinsert needle and bring it straight down, pulling needle and floss completely through to back of fabric. Keep floss flat but do not pull tight. For even stitches, keep tension consistent throughout.

Carrying Floss: To carry floss, weave it under previously worked stitches on back. Do not carry floss across any fabric that is not or will not be stitched. Loose strands, especially dark ones, will show through fabric.

page 80

Cleaning Completed Work: When stitching is complete, soak finished piece in cold water with mild soap for 5 to 10 minutes; rinse thoroughly. Roll work in towel to remove excess water; do not wring. Place work facedown on dry towel and press with warm iron until work is dry.

Note: If design piece includes metallic threads or blending filaments, place a clean, dry cloth between fabric and iron. Press gently.

WASTE CANVAS

Waste canvas is a coarse fabric used as a guide for stitching on fabrics other than even-weaves.

Stitch over 1 unit (2 threads). Cut waste canvas at least 1" larger on all sides than finished design size. Baste waste canvas to fabric to be stitched.

When stitching is complete, use spray bottle to dampen stitched area with cold water.

Using tweezers, pull out waste canvas threads 1 at a time. Pull out all threads running in 1 direction first; then pull out remaining threads. Let stitching dry; then place facedown on towel and iron.

PERFORATED PAPER

Cut perforated paper at least 1" larger on all sides than finished design size. Stitch over 1 mesh (see Diagram below). Be careful when pulling floss; too much tension can tear the small spaces between perforations. When stitching is complete, trim paper to 1 hole outside design, being careful not to cut into any hole holding a stitch.

Diagram

SEWING HINTS

Bias Strips: In this book, bias strips are used to make corded piping. To cut bias strips, fold fabric at 45° angle to grain of fabric and crease. Cut along crease. Cut strips to measure width indicated in Directions, cutting parallel to first cutting line. Ends of bias strips should be cut on grain of fabric. With right sides facing, place ends of strips together as shown and stitch with ¼" seam (see Diagram below). Press seam open and trim seam allowance even with strip. Continue to piece strips until they are length indicated in Directions.

Bias Strips

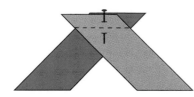

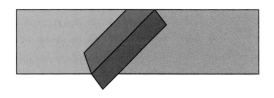

Corded Piping: From pieced bias strip and cording, cut length indicated in Directions. With wrong sides facing and raw edges aligned, fold pieced strip in half lengthwise, encasing cording in fold. Stitch close to cord to secure.

Gathering: Machine-stitch 2 parallel rows of long stitches, ¼" and ½" from raw edge of fabric. Leave thread ends at least 3" long. Pull bobbin threads and gather to fit desired length. Disperse fullness evenly and secure threads.

Marking Fabric: Always use dressmaker's pen or chalk to mark on fabric. It will wash out when finished piece is cleaned.

Slipstitch: This stitch is an almost invisible stitch. Use it to secure folded edges of fabric together or folded edge to base fabric (see Diagram below).

Slipstitch

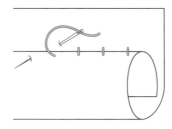

Tassels: For a decorative tassel, wrap floss or ribbon around cardboard piece to make thick bundle (see Diagram A). Thread needle with length of same color floss. Slide needle under 1 end of ribbon bundle (see Diagram B). Pull needle free and tie floss in very tight knot around bundle. Cut bundle at end opposite knot (see Diagram C). Wrap separate length of floss several times around bundle and knot to secure (see Diagram D). Trim ends of tassel even.

page 68

Making a Tassel

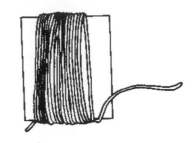

Diagram A

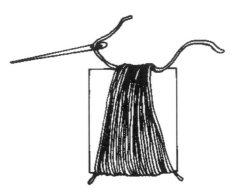

Diagram B

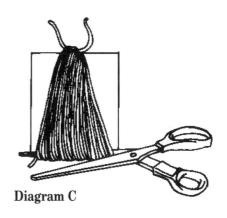

Diagram C

Diagram D

136

COMMON STITCHES

Cross-Stitch: Make 1 cross for each symbol on graph. Bring needle up at A, down at B, up at C, and down at D (see Diagram below).

For vertical rows, complete each stitch individually (see Diagram below).

For horizontal rows, stitch from left to right to make half-crosses and then back to complete stitches (see Diagram below). All understitches must slant in 1 direction and all overstitches must slant in opposite direction.

Cross-Stitch

Cross-Stitch: Vertical Row

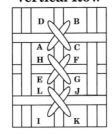

Cross-Stitch: Horizontal Row

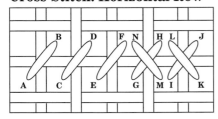

Three-quarter Stitch: A three-quarter stitch is used to make a curved line. It is indicated on graph when symbol fills only half of square (see Diagrams at top of next column). If you are working over 1 thread, short understitch will pierce fabric thread; if you are working over 2 threads, it will slip through hole between 2 threads. Make long stitch in direction of slanted line on graph. Long stitch is always overstitch.

Three-quarter Stitch

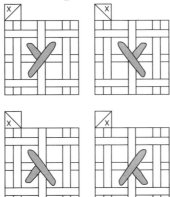

Three-quarter Stitch (dominant color): When 2 symbols occupy single square on graph, make a three-quarter stitch and a quarter stitch to fill square. Use three-quarter stitch to express dominant line or color (see Diagram below).

Three-quarter Stitch: Dominant Color

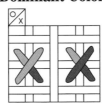

Backstitch: Complete all cross-stitches before working backstitches or other accent stitches. Work from right to left with 1 strand of floss (unless otherwise indicated). Bring needle up at A, down at B, and up at C (see Diagram below). Going back down at A, continue in this manner.

Backstitch

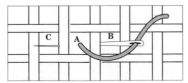

Beadwork: Attach bead to fabric with diagonal stitch, working from lower left to upper right. Secure bead by returning thread through bead, from lower right to upper left. When working in rows, complete a row of diagonal stitches before returning to secure all beads (see Diagram below).

Beadwork

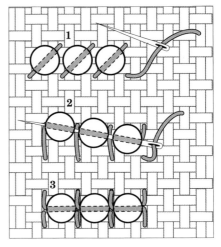

French Knot: Bring needle up at A. Wrap floss around needle twice (unless otherwise indicated). Insert needle beside A, pulling floss until it fits snugly around needle. Pull needle through to back (see Diagram below).

French Knot

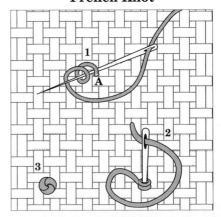

137

Special Stitches

These enlarged diagrams will help you work the more technical stitches.

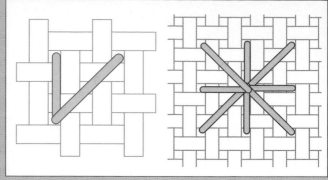

Algerian Eye Stitch

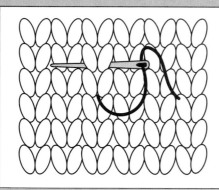

Couching

Couching with Cross-Stitch

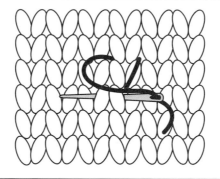
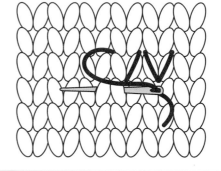

Duplicate Stitch

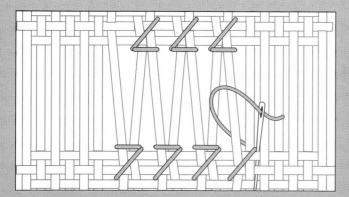

Serpentine Hemstitch

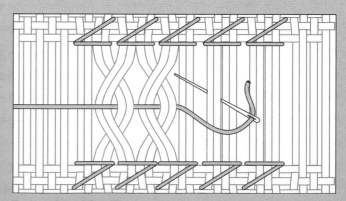

Twisted Ladder Hemstitch

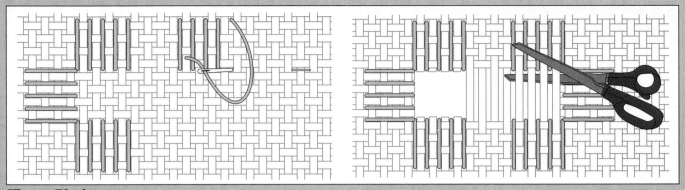

Kloster Blocks

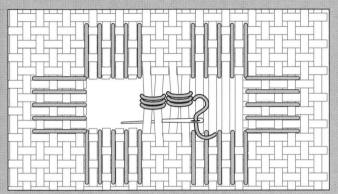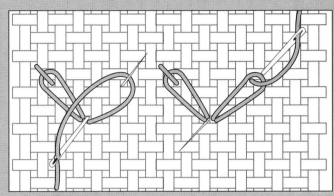

Kloster Blocks with Figure-Eight Wraps

Lazy Daisy Stitch

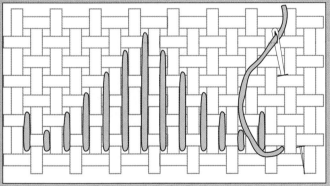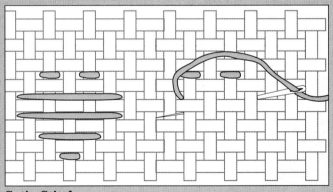

Long Stitch

Satin Stitch

Smyrna Cross

Framing Ideas

Once you have completed your cross-stitch piece, it is important to find a mat and a frame that will enhance its beauty. These are our professional secrets for perfect results.

PREPARE DESIGN PIECE

Lacing is the process of mounting a design piece on mat board with strong thread; it is the best way to prepare cross-stitch for framing. Better frame shops will lace needlework, but it is often quite expensive.

To lace the design piece yourself, you will need the following tools and materials:

Completed cross-stitch piece
Liquid ravel preventer
2 pieces of paper (at least size of design piece)
Straight pins
Mat board or foam-core board for backing
Ruler
Craft knife
Sewing needle and thread
Large-eyed blunt needle
Spool of carpet thread

1. Clean, dry, and press design piece (see General Instructions). Apply liquid ravel preventer to edges of fabric and let dry.

2. To decide how much fabric should show around design, create a temporary mat. Place design piece right side up on clean surface. Referring to **Diagram 1**: Cut 2 right angles from paper. Use these to frame design piece until satisfied with effect. Before removing paper, mark position of temporary mat window with pins. Measure and mark with pins desired width of mat. Cut mat board backing to fit overall size of mat. Remove mat window pins.

3. Referring to **Diagram 2**: Place design piece right side down. Align backing edges with pins. Remove top pin and fold excess fabric over top edge of backing. Following a horizontal thread, push pins ½" apart through fabric into edge of backing. Leave corners loose. Repeat with bottom, left, and right edges, keeping tension even all around. Do not pull fabric so taut that backing bends or fabric weave is distorted.

4. Miter each corner; pin (**Diagram 3**). Working on 1 side at a time, remove pins from edge of backing and push them into edge of fabric at 45° angle, keeping fabric taut (**Diagram 4**). Beginning in outer corner, stitch each mitered corner together (**Diagram 5**). Remove all remaining pins.

5. Draw guideline ⅝" from raw edges of fabric. Thread large-eyed needle from spool of carpet thread; do not cut or knot thread. Referring to **Diagram 6**: Begin in right corner of top margin and draw thread down through fabric at guideline. Draw thread up

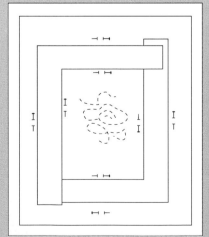

Diagram 1
Mark temporary mat window.

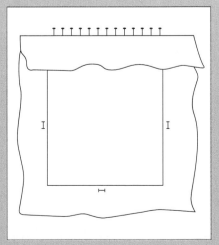

Diagram 2
Pin fabric to edges of backing.

through bottom margin and down again through top margin, following a horizontal thread. Continue lacing in this manner until complete.

Cut off needle and knot thread to secure but leave thread attached to spool. Working backward toward spool, pull each lacing taut without distorting fabric weave or causing backing to bow. Cut thread from spool; secure. Repeat to lace fabric from side to side.

DECORATIVE MATS

The color and texture of a mat should complement the piece without detracting from it. As a general rule, designs should be matted with equal unstitched space at the top and the sides, with ⅛" to ½" extra space at the bottom. This prevents the piece from looking top-heavy. Have a professional framer cut your mat, as cutting your own can be difficult. After the mat is cut, customize it for your cross-stitch piece.

• Layer 2 or more mats in graduated sizes and contrasting colors (see pages 36 and 58). If desired, when layering 2 mats, have framer cut designs out of top mat (see pages 106 and 114).

• Spray-paint mat in several different colors to complement subtle gradations of variegated thread (see page 83).

• Drizzle lines of acrylic paint onto mat (see page 58) or splatter-paint mat. Dilute paint with water in disposable container. Dip small paintbrush into paint and let paint drizzle onto mat. Or dab old toothbrush into paint and pull your finger or blunt knife across bristles to splatter.

• Use dimensional paint to make raised dots on mat (see page 96).

• Attach unique items to mat that complement design (see page 66).

• Purchase mat board covered with printed or raised fabric textures (see page 90). To make your own, coat mat with spray adhesive and smooth fabric onto it. Cut fabric, leaving ¼" to ½" margin inside mat window and outside edges. Clip corners; fold fabric to back and glue.

page 16

CREATIVE FRAMES

The frame is the finishing touch for your design piece.

Wooden frames go well with cross-stitch and are most suitable for creative customizing. Look for interesting frames at garage sales and secondhand stores. Here are several ideas for embellishing your frame:

• Paint unfinished frame with acrylic paint or spray paint. For glossier look, coat frame with acrylic gloss finish.

• For an antique look, paint base coat on frame; let dry. Paint over base coat with complementary color; let dry. Brush frame gently with wire brush (see page 40).

• Decorate with random patterns such as dots or stripes. Or pull motifs from design piece and paint freehand on frame (see page 16).

• Glue purchased wooden cutouts to frame. Stain or paint cutouts first if desired (see page 130).

• Attach handles to frame and make a unique tray. Paint handles same color as frame (see page 55) or polish metal handles (see page 64).

Cross-stitch is often framed without a sheet of glass. If you do use glass, do not let it touch design piece as it will flatten stitches.

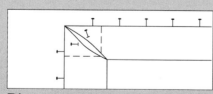

Diagram 3
Miter corners.

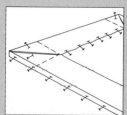

Diagram 4
Pin fabric to back.

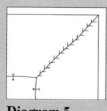

Diagram 5
Stitch mitered corners.

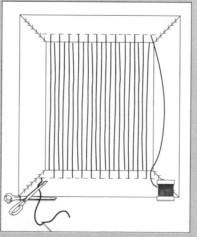

Diagram 6
Lace design piece.

Cover Design

SAMPLE
Stitched on antique white 28-count
Cashel Linen over 2 threads, the
finished design size is 10" x 13".
The fabric was cut 17" x 20".

FABRICS
11-count
14-count
18-count
22-count

DESIGN SIZES
13¾" x 16⅞"
10¾" x 13¼"
8⅜" x 10¼"
6⅞" x 8⅜"

142

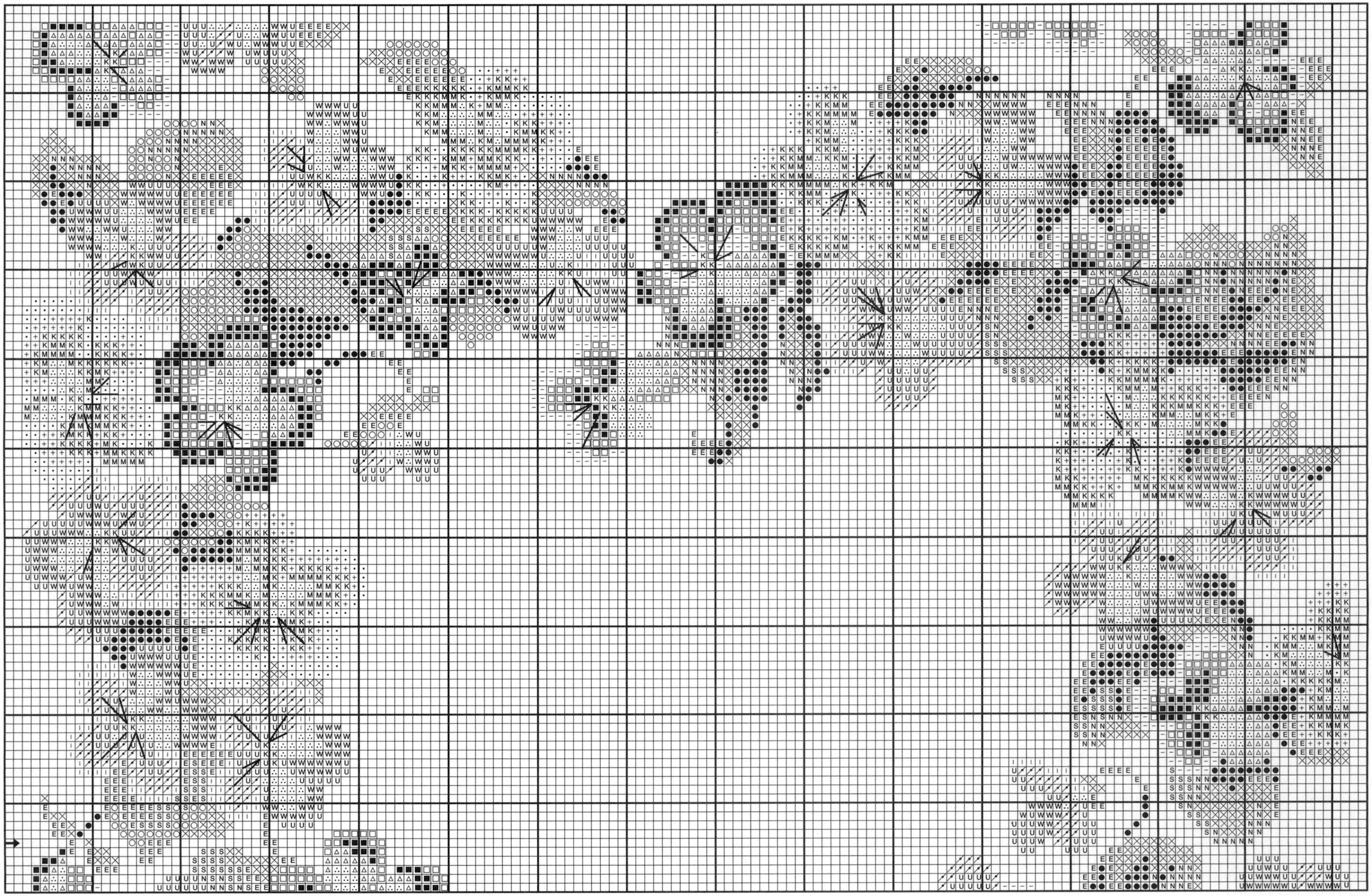